Trevor Senior

GW00601334

ESSENTIALS

Edexcel
GCSE Maths
Foundation Tier
Revision Guide

Contents

		Maths B Unit Reference	Revised

Contents

		Maths B Unit Reference	Revised

Basic Number Work

Place Value

Numbers are made up of **digits**, e.g. the number 2475 has the digits 2, 4, 7 and 5.

The position of a digit in a number is called its **place value**.

Thousands	Hundreds	Tens	Units
2	4	7	5

In the number 2475:
- the value of the 2 is 2000
- the value of the 4 is 400
- the value of the 7 is 70, and so on.

2475 written in words is two thousand, four hundred and seventy-five.

Example

a) Write the number 2012 in words.

Solution

2012 is written as two thousand and twelve.

b) Write the number four hundred and seven in digits.

Solution

Four hundred and seven is written as 407.

Adding and Subtracting Whole Numbers

To add or subtract whole numbers, line up the digits in place value order.

Example

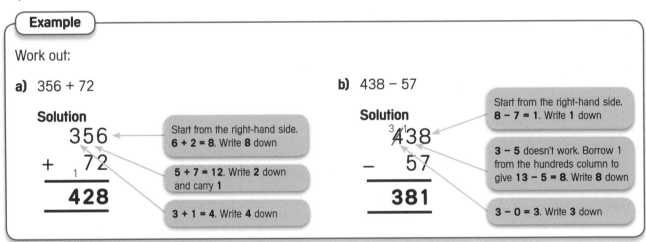

Work out:

a) 356 + 72

Solution

$$\begin{array}{r} 356 \\ +\ \ 72 \\ _1 \\ \hline 428 \end{array}$$

Start from the right-hand side. **6 + 2 = 8**. Write **8** down

5 + 7 = 12. Write **2** down and carry **1**

3 + 1 = 4. Write **4** down

b) 438 − 57

Solution

$$\begin{array}{r} {}^3\!\!\!\not 4\,{}^1\!3\,8 \\ -\ \ 57 \\ \hline 381 \end{array}$$

Start from the right-hand side. **8 − 7 = 1**. Write **1** down

3 − 5 doesn't work. Borrow 1 from the hundreds column to give **13 − 5 = 8**. Write **8** down

3 − 0 = 3. Write **3** down

Multiplying and Dividing Whole Numbers by Powers of 10

To multiply a whole number by 10, 100 or 1000:
1. move the digits one, two or three places to the left
2. fill the empty place-value columns with zeros.

For example, 38 × 10 = 380, 38 × 100 = 3800, 38 × 1000 = 38 000, and so on.

To divide a whole number by 10, 100 or 1000:
1. move the digits one, two or three places to the right
2. remember the decimal point.

For example, 38 ÷ 10 = 3.8, 38 ÷ 100 = 0.38, 38 ÷ 1000 = 0.038, and so on.

Basic Number Work

Long Multiplication and Long Division of Whole Numbers

To use **long multiplication**:

1. multiply by the units digit
2. multiply by the tens digit, and so on.

To use **long division**:

1. divide
2. multiply
3. subtract
4. bring down.

Example

Work out 364 × 14

Solution A

$$
\begin{array}{r}
364 \\
\times \quad 14 \\
\hline
145\overset{2}{}\overset{1}{6} \\
3640 \\
\hline
5\overset{1}{0}96 \\
\hline
\end{array}
$$

Working out 364 × 4

Working out 364 × 10

Adding the two multiplications together

Solution B (Grid method)

×	**300**	**60**	**4**	
10	3000	600	40	3640
4	1200	240	16	1456

$$4200 + 840 + 56 = 5096$$

Example 1

Work out 312 ÷ 12

Solution

$$
\begin{array}{r}
26 \\
12\overline{)312} \\
24 \\
\hline
72 \\
72 \\
\hline
0 \\
\end{array}
$$

- **12** doesn't divide into **3** so move on.
- **31** ÷ **12** goes **2** times. **12** × **2** = **24**. Write **24** below **31** and subtract to give **7**.
- Bring down the **2**. **12** into **72** goes **6** times. **12** × **6** = **72**.

So 312 ÷ 12 = 26

Example 2

Work out 630 ÷ 18

Solution

$$
\begin{array}{r}
35 \\
18\overline{)630} \\
54 \\
\hline
90 \\
\end{array}
$$

Divide 63 by 18

3 × 18 = 54

63 − 54 = 9. Bring down the '0', then divide 90 by 18 (= 5)

So 630 ÷ 18 = 35

Quick Test

1. Write the number one thousand, two hundred and eighty in digits.
2. What is the value of the digit 5 in the number 3514?
3. Work out each of the following:

   a) 439 + 814　　b) 281 − 147　　c) 234 × 5　　d) 612 ÷ 4

Positive and Negative Numbers

Positive and Negative Numbers

Positive numbers are numbers greater than zero and **negative numbers** are numbers less than zero. These can be shown on a number line.

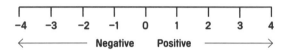

An **integer** is a whole number. It can be positive, negative or zero. −5, 0 and 3 are examples of integers.

Example

What temperature is shown on this thermometer?

Solution

The temperature is −2°C.

Adding and Subtracting Integers

You can use a number line to help you **add** or **subtract** numbers:

- Adding a positive number increases the answer (→)
- Subtracting a positive number decreases the answer (←)

You can also use a number line to help you **add** or **subtract** negative numbers:

- Adding a negative number decreases the answer (←)
- Subtracting a negative number increases the answer (→)

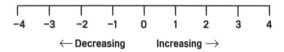

Example 1

Work out 3 − 5.

Solution

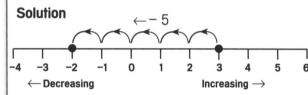

Starting at 3 and decreasing by 5 gives:

3 − 5 = −2

Example 2

Work out 2 − (−4).

Solution

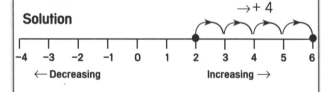

Starting at 2 and increasing by 4 gives:

2 − (−4) = 2 + 4 = 6 ⟵ − − = +

Example 3

Work out 5 + (−6).

Solution

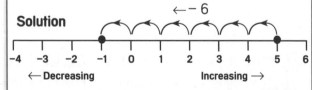

Starting at 5 and decreasing by 6 gives:

5 + (−6) = 5 − 6 = −1 ⟵ + − = −

Key Words   Positive number • Negative number • Integer

Example 4

Here is a bank statement showing some credits (money put in) and some debits (money taken out):

Complete the balance column.

Solution

On 18/06/12 £64.30 is paid out for petrol, so the balance is:

£189.70 − £64.30 = £125.40

On 19/06/12 £45.21 is paid in by cheque, so the balance is:

£125.40 + £45.21 = £170.61

Multiplying and Dividing Integers

You need to remember the following when multiplying or dividing two numbers:

- If the signs are the **same**, the answer is **positive**,
  i.e: **+ × + = +**   **+ ÷ + = +**
        − × − = +   **− ÷ − = +**

- If the signs are **different**, the answer is **negative**,
  i.e: **+ × − = −**   **+ ÷ − = −**
        − × + = −   **− ÷ + = −**

Example

Work out:

a) 7 × −8

   Solution
   7 × −8 = −56 ← [+ × − = −]

b) −9 × −2

   Solution
   −9 × −2 = 18 ← [− × − = +]

c) −30 ÷ 6

   Solution
   −30 ÷ 6 = −5 ← [− ÷ + = −]

d) −25 ÷ −5

   Solution
   −25 ÷ −5 = 5 ← [− ÷ − = +]

Quick Test

 1 Work out each of the following:

   a) −3 − 4
   b) 7 − (−2)
   c) −8 + 6
   d) −1 + (−1)
   e) −4 × −3
   f) 9 × −2
   g) −12 ÷ 2
   h) −21 ÷ −7

Rounding

Rounding and Approximation

Numbers are **rounded**:
- to **estimate** the answer to a calculation using **approximate** values
- to give a sensible answer.

Example

Jack sees batteries advertised for £1.49 each. He has £10. How many can he buy?

Solution

> **Problem Solving**
>
> Use a sensible estimate to make this type of calculation easier.

Using £1.50, he would get 2 for £3, so he can buy 6 for £9. He doesn't have enough to buy any more.

Estimating Values of Calculations

When you approximate the value of a number always work to 1 **significant figure** (see page 9). For example, 18.8 approximates to 20 using 1 significant figure.

Example 1

Use approximations to estimate the answer to 47×201.

Solution

$47 = 50$ to 1 significant figure and $201 = 200$ to 1 significant figure

$50 \times 200 = 10\,000$

So 47×201 is approximately $10\,000$.

Example 2

Use approximations to estimate the answer to $\dfrac{5020}{4.9 \times 20.8}$

Solution

Rounding each number to 1 significant figure:

$\dfrac{5000}{5 \times 20} = 50$

Example 3

Use approximations to estimate the value of $\dfrac{19.7 \times 30.1}{0.59}$

Solution

$\dfrac{19.7 \times 30.1}{0.59}$ is approximately $\dfrac{20 \times 30}{0.6}$

Rounding each number to 1 significant figure

$\dfrac{20 \times 30}{0.6} = \dfrac{600}{0.6}$

To remove the decimal from this calculation, multiply the numerator and denominator by 10

$\dfrac{6000}{6} = 1000$

So $\dfrac{19.7 \times 30.1}{0.59}$ is approximately 1000.

Key Words Rounding • Estimate • Approximation • Significant figure

Decimal Places

Look at the number **27.35083**

To round to 1 **decimal place**, look at the **second** decimal place:

- If the second decimal place has a value of 5 or more, round up the number in the first decimal place.
- If the second decimal place has a value of less than 5, leave the number in the first decimal place unchanged.

To round to **2 decimal places**, look at the **third** decimal place, and so on.

So:

- 27.3 | **5**083 = 27.4 to 1 decimal place (i.e. 3 rounds up to 4)
- 27.35 | **0**83 = 27.35 to 2 decimal places (i.e. 5 stays unchanged)
- 27.350 | **8**3 = 27.351 to 3 decimal places (i.e. 0 rounds up to 1).

Significant Figures

The first **significant figure** is the first non-zero digit from the left.

Look again at the number **27.35083**

To round to 1 significant figure, look at the **second** significant figure:

- If the second significant figure has a value of 5 or more, round up the first significant figure.
- If the second significant figure has a value of less than 5, leave the first significant figure unchanged.

To round to **2 significant figures**, look at the **third** significant figure, and so on.

Use zeros to keep the place value of the significant figures.

So:

- 2 | **7**.35083 = 30 to 1 significant figure (i.e. 2 rounds up to 3 and put a zero in the units column)
- 27. | **3**5083 = 27 to 2 significant figures (i.e. 7 stays unchanged)
- 27.3 | **5**083 = 27.4 to 3 significant figures (i.e. 3 rounds up to 4).

Example

Write the number 0.03053 to 2 significant figures.

Solution

The first significant figure is the digit 3.

So 0.030 | **5**3 = 0.031 to 2 significant figures.

0 is followed by a 5, so round up to 1

The leading zeros are used to keep the place value of the significant figures

Quick Test

1. Round the following numbers to:
   i) 1 decimal place
   ii) 2 decimal places
   iii) 1 significant figure
   iv) 2 significant figures.
   a) 18.725 b) 0.0725 c) 2436.518

2. Use approximations to estimate the value of each of the following:
   a) $\dfrac{71.2 + 28.8}{9.5}$
   b) $\dfrac{4.15 \times 38.7}{7.69}$
   c) $\dfrac{99.9 \times 5.87}{0.29}$

Multiples and Factors

Order of Operations

BIDMAS is a way of remembering the order to carry out operations. Simplify **brackets** first, then work out any **indices** (powers) and finally **divide**, **multiply**, **add** and **subtract** in that order:

- **B**rackets, e.g. $2 \times (8 + 3) = 2 \times 11 = 22$
- **I**ndices (or powers), e.g. $3^2 \times (7 - 2)^2 = 3^2 \times 5^2$
  $= 9 \times 25 = 225$
- **D**ivision, e.g. $3 + 4^2 \div 2 = 3 + 16 \div 2 = 3 + 8 = 11$
- **M**ultiplication, e.g. $3 \times 8 \div 2 + 1$
  $= 3 \times 4 + 1 = 12 + 1 = 13$
- **A**ddition, e.g. $3 + 5 \times 4^2 = 3 + 5 \times 16$
  $= 3 + 80 = 83$
- **S**ubtraction, e.g. $3 \times 10 \div 2 - 1 + 4$
  $= 3 \times 5 - 1 + 4 = 15 - 1 + 4 = 18$

Number Facts

You should know these sets of numbers:
- **Even numbers**: 2, 4, 6, 8, 10…
- **Odd numbers**: 1, 3, 5, 7, 9…
- **Prime numbers**: 2, 3, 5, 7, 11…

Multiples of a number are found by multiplying the number by another **integer**, e.g.:
- multiples of 3 are 3, 6, 9, 12, 15…
- multiples of 7 are 7, 14, 21, 28, 35…

Factors of a number are all the whole numbers that divide into it exactly, e.g.:
- factors of 17 are 1 and 17
- factors of 18 are 1, 2, 3, 6, 9 and 18
- factors of 25 are 1, 5 and 25.

N.B. Prime numbers only have two factors – the number itself and 1.

Product of Prime Factors

Prime factors are factors of a number that are also prime.

Example

Write 24 as a **product** of prime factors.

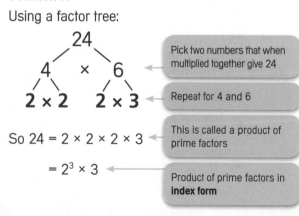

Solution A

Using a factor tree:

Pick two numbers that when multiplied together give 24

Repeat for 4 and 6

So $24 = 2 \times 2 \times 2 \times 3$

This is called a product of prime factors

$= 2^3 \times 3$

Product of prime factors in **index form**

Solution B

Using prime factor decomposition:

2 is prime and is a factor of 24, so $24 \div 2 = 12$

2 is also a factor of 12, so $12 \div 2 = 6$

2 is also a factor of 6, so $6 \div 2 = 3$

So $24 = 2 \times 2 \times 2 \times 3$

$= 2^3 \times 3$

3 is prime and is a factor of itself, so $3 \div 3 = 1$

Least Common Multiple and Highest Common Factor

Least Common Multiple (LCM)

The **least common multiple** (or lowest common multiple) of two numbers is the lowest number that is in the multiplication tables of both numbers.

Example 1

Work out the least common multiple of 5 and 8.

Solution

Multiples of 5 are:
5, 10, 15, 20, 25, 30, 35, (40), 45...

Multiples of 8 are:
8, 16, 24, 32, (40), 48, 56...

40 is the lowest number in both lists, so 40 is the least common multiple.

Example 2

Work out the highest common factor of 24 and 40.

Solution

The factors of 24 are:
1, 2, 3, 4, 6, (8), 12 and 24.

The factors of 40 are:
1, 2, 4, 5, (8), 10, 20 and 40.

8 is the highest number in both lists, so 8 is the highest common factor.

Highest Common Factor (HCF)

The **highest common factor** of two numbers is the highest number that divides into both numbers.

Example 3

The least common multiple of two numbers is 24. The highest common factor of the same two numbers is 4.

Work out the two numbers.

Solution

Problem Solving
Break this type of question into several steps. Start by listing the multiples of 4 as you know that 4 is a factor of both numbers.

Multiples of 4 are 4, 8, 12, 16, 20, 24...

Numbers in this list which are factors of 24 are 8, 12 and 24.

The two numbers must be 8 and 12 to satisfy both conditions.

Quick Test

1. Work out the following:
   a) $(6 - 4) \times (5 + 2)$ **b)** $5^3 + 50 \div 10$ **c)** $3^2 + 4^2 + 5^2 \times 2$
2. Write 60 as a product of prime factors. Give your answer in index form.
3. Work out the least common multiple of the following:
   a) 8 and 10   **b)** 4 and 7   **c)** 6 and 9
4. Work out the highest common factor of the following:
   a) 20 and 28   **b)** 15 and 25   **c)** 12 and 30

Fractions

Equivalent Fractions

Equivalent fractions are fractions that can be simplified (cancelled down) to the same value.

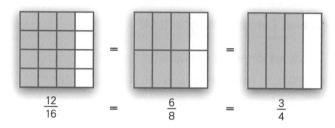

$$\frac{12}{16} = \frac{6}{8} = \frac{3}{4}$$

Adding and Subtracting Fractions

To add or subtract fractions they must have the same **denominator**.

Example 1

Work out $\frac{3}{4} + \frac{1}{5}$

Solution

$\frac{3}{4} + \frac{1}{5} = \frac{15}{20} + \frac{4}{20}$

$= \frac{19}{20}$

> 20 is the least common multiple of 4 and 5.
> $\frac{3}{4} = \frac{15}{20}$ and $\frac{1}{5} = \frac{4}{20}$

Example 2

Work out $2\frac{2}{3} + 1\frac{1}{2}$

Solution

$2\frac{2}{3} + 1\frac{1}{2} = 2 + 1 + \frac{2}{3} + \frac{1}{2}$

$= 3 + \frac{4}{6} + \frac{3}{6}$

$= 3 + 1\frac{1}{6} = 4\frac{1}{6}$

> $= 3 + \frac{7}{6}$

Example 3

Work out $4\frac{1}{4} - 2\frac{1}{2}$

Solution A

$4\frac{1}{4} - 2\frac{1}{2} = 4 - 2 + \frac{1}{4} - \frac{1}{2}$

$= 2 + \frac{1}{4} - \frac{2}{4}$

$= 1\frac{3}{4}$

> $= 2 - \frac{1}{4}$

Solution B

$4\frac{1}{4} - 2\frac{1}{2} = \frac{17}{4} - \frac{5}{2}$

$= \frac{17}{4} - \frac{10}{4}$

$= \frac{7}{4}$

$= 1\frac{3}{4}$

> Here we are changing the mixed numbers to improper fractions. There are four quarters or two halves in 1. So, $4\frac{1}{4}$ is 17 quarters and $2\frac{1}{2}$ is 5 halves

Multiplying Fractions

To multiply fractions:

1. change any **mixed numbers** to **improper fractions**
2. multiply the **numerators** together
3. multiply the denominators together
4. simplify the answer if possible.

Example 1

Work out $\frac{3}{4} \times \frac{3}{5}$

Solution

$\frac{3}{4} \times \frac{3}{5} = \frac{9}{20}$

Example 2

Work out $2\frac{2}{3} \times 1\frac{1}{5}$

Solution

$2\frac{2}{3} \times 1\frac{1}{5} = \frac{8}{3} \times \frac{6}{5}$

$= \frac{8}{\cancel{3}_1} \times \frac{\cancel{6}^2}{5}$

$= \frac{16}{5}$

$= 3\frac{1}{5}$

> Simplify by cancelling by 3

Key Words   Equivalent fraction • Denominator • Mixed number • Improper fraction • Numerator

Dividing Fractions

To divide fractions:

1. change any mixed numbers to improper fractions
2. turn the second fraction upside down and change the division to multiplication
3. do the multiplication as shown on page 12.

Example 1

Work out $\frac{5}{6} \div \frac{3}{5}$

Solution

$\frac{5}{6} \div \frac{3}{5} = \frac{5}{6} \times \frac{5}{3}$

$= \frac{25}{18}$

$= 1\frac{7}{18}$

Example 2

Work out $1\frac{1}{4} \div 2\frac{1}{3}$

Solution

$1\frac{1}{4} \div 2\frac{1}{3} = \frac{5}{4} \div \frac{7}{3}$

$= \frac{5}{4} \times \frac{3}{7}$

$= \frac{15}{28}$

Fractions of Quantities

To calculate a fraction of a quantity, multiply the fraction by the quantity.

To write a quantity as a fraction of another quantity:

1. match the units
2. write the fraction and simplify.

Example 1

$\frac{3}{4}$ of the 28 students in a class are boys. How many are girls?

Solution

Problem Solving
You can either work out $\frac{1}{4}$ of 28 for the number of girls or $\frac{3}{4}$ of 28 for the number of boys and then subtract this from the total number of students.

$\frac{3}{4}$ of $28 = \frac{3}{4} \times 28$

$= \frac{3}{\cancel{4}1} \times \frac{\cancel{28}^7}{1} = 21$

There are 21 boys, so there are:

$28 - 21 = 7$ girls

Example 2

Write 30 cm as a fraction of 1 metre.

Solution

1 metre = 100 cm ← Make the units the same

So 30 cm as a fraction of 1 metre is $\frac{30 \text{ cm}}{100 \text{ cm}} = \frac{3}{10}$

Example 3

In two tests, Nicholas gets 13 out of 15 and 16 out of 20.

Which is the better score?

Solution

Problem Solving
To compare the two scores, one way is to write them as fractions with common denominators. Then compare the numerators.

13 out of 15 is $\frac{13}{15} = \frac{52}{60}$ ← Multiply the numerator and denominator by 4

16 out of 20 is $\frac{16}{20} = \frac{48}{60}$ ← Multiply the numerator and denominator by 3

So 13 out of 15 is the better score.

Quick Test

1. Work out:
   a) $1\frac{1}{4} + 3\frac{1}{3}$ b) $2\frac{3}{5} - 1\frac{1}{4}$ c) $1\frac{1}{2} \times 1\frac{1}{3}$ d) $3\frac{4}{5} \div 2\frac{1}{6}$
2. Work out $\frac{2}{3}$ of £60.
3. Write 50 grams as a fraction of 1 kilogram. (*Hint: 1 kg = 1000 g*)

Decimals

Place Value and Ordering Decimals

The place value headings can be extended for decimals.

Thousands	Hundreds	Tens	Units	Decimal Point	Tenths	Hundredths	Thousandths
2	4	7	5	.	9	3	8

In the number 2475.938:
- the value of the 9 is $\frac{9}{10}$
- the value of the 3 is $\frac{3}{100}$
- the value of the 8 is $\frac{8}{1000}$

To put decimals into order from smallest to biggest:

1 rewrite the numbers with the same number of decimal places by inserting zeros

2 order them by the whole number parts

3 order them by the tenths, then the hundredths, and so on.

Example

Write these numbers in order, smallest first:

23.41   23.14   23.4   22.04   24.16   23.61   22.4

Solution

> Rewriting the numbers with two decimal places

23.41   23.14   23.40   22.04   24.16   23.61   22.40

> Ordering by whole numbers (22, 23, 24)

22.04   22.40   23.41   23.14   23.40   23.61   24.16

> Ordering by tenths (23.14 and 23.41)

22.04   22.40   23.14   23.41   23.40   23.61   24.16

> Ordering by hundredths (23.40 and 23.41)

22.04   22.40   23.14   23.40   23.41   23.61   24.16

> Rewriting as in the question

22.04   22.4   23.14   23.4   23.41   23.61   24.16

Terminating and Recurring Decimals

A **terminating decimal** is a decimal that has a finite number of digits.

For example, $\frac{1}{2}$ = 0.5 or $\frac{1}{4}$ = 0.25

A **recurring decimal** has an infinite number of digits in a repeating pattern.

For example, $\frac{1}{3}$ = 0.333 333… or $\frac{2}{11}$ = 0.181 818…

These are written as $0.\dot{3}$ and $0.\dot{1}\dot{8}$

Converting Fractions into Recurring Decimals

To convert a fraction into a decimal, divide the numerator by the denominator.

Example 1

Use a calculator to convert $\frac{2}{7}$ to a recurring decimal.

Solution

2 ÷ 7 is 0.285 714 285 714… = $0.\dot{2}8571\dot{4}$

Example 2

Convert $\frac{2}{7}$ into a recurring decimal without using a calculator.

Solution

$$\frac{0.2\ 8\ 5\ 7\ 1\ 4\ 2…}{7\,|\,2.0\,{}^6 0\,{}^4 0\,{}^5 0\,{}^1 0\,{}^3 0\,{}^2 0…} = 0.\dot{2}8571\dot{4}$$

Addition and Subtraction of Decimals

To add or subtract decimals you must:

1. line up the decimal points underneath each other
2. put the decimal point of the answer underneath the other decimal points.

Example

Work out:

a) 5.38 + 7.56   **b)** 8.1 − 6.3

Solution

```
   5.38
+  7.56
  12.94
```

Solution

```
  ⁷8̶.¹1
−  6.3
   1.8
```

Multiplication of Decimals

To multiply a decimal number by another decimal number:

1. complete the multiplication as if the decimal points weren't there
2. count the total number of decimal places in the two numbers
3. put the decimal point in the answer so that it has the same number of decimal places as the total for the two numbers.

Example

Work out 2.34 × 5.1

Solution

```
      2.34        ← Three decimal places
   ×   5.1
      234         ← 234 × 1
    11700         ← 234 × 50
    11.934        ← Three decimal places
```

Division of Decimals

To divide a decimal number by a whole number, put the decimal point of the answer above the decimal in the question.

To divide a decimal number by a decimal number:

1. count the decimal places of the number you're dividing by
2. multiply both numbers by 10, 100 or 1000 depending whether it's 1, 2 or 3 decimal places, etc.
3. divide as before using long or short division.

Example 1

Work out 13.2 ÷ 6

Solution

```
      2.2
  6 ) 13.2       ← Remember to take the
      12            decimal point up into
       1 2          the answer
       1 2
          0
```

So 13.2 ÷ 6 = 2.2

Example 2

Work out 18.312 ÷ 0.6 ← One decimal place so multiply both numbers by 10

Solution

18.312 ÷ 0.6 is the same as 183.12 ÷ 6

```
        30.52
  6 ) 183.³1²2     ← Using short division
```

So 18.312 ÷ 0.6 = 30.52

Quick Test

1. Change these fractions to decimals:
   a) $\frac{2}{5}$ **b)** $\frac{4}{9}$ **c)** $\frac{3}{13}$
2. 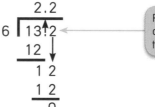 Put these decimals in order, smallest first:
   9.87 10.02 9.78 10.9 10.3 10.39
3. Work out the following:
   a) 35.9 + 18.7   **b)** 2.51 − 1.7
   c) 3.42 × 25   **d)** 6.71 ÷ 1.1

Percentages

Simple Percentages

A **percentage** is an amount 'out of 100', e.g. 32% is the same as $\frac{32}{100}$ or 0.32

You should know these conversions:

Percentage	Fraction	Decimal
50%	$\frac{1}{2}$	0.5
25%	$\frac{1}{4}$	0.25
75%	$\frac{3}{4}$	0.75
10%	$\frac{1}{10}$	0.1
$33\frac{1}{3}$%	$\frac{1}{3}$	0.333...
$66\frac{2}{3}$%	$\frac{2}{3}$	0.666...

Example 1

Convert 72% to a fraction in its simplest form.

Solution

72% is the same as $\frac{72}{100} = \frac{18}{25}$ ← Cancelling by 4

Example 2

Convert $\frac{7}{20}$ to a percentage.

Solution

$\frac{7}{20}$ is the same as $\frac{7}{20} \times 100 = 35\%$ ← Cancelling down 100 and 20 to give 7 × 5

Calculating a Percentage of a Quantity

To calculate a percentage of a quantity:

1. change the percentage to a fraction or a decimal fraction
2. calculate the fraction of the quantity.

Example

Work out 80% of 200 grams.

Solution

80% of 200 grams is $\frac{80}{100} \times 200 = 160$ grams

One Quantity as a Percentage of Another Quantity

To express one quantity as a percentage of another quantity:

1. make sure both quantities are in the same units
2. express the quantity as a fraction of the other quantity
3. change the fraction to a percentage.

Example

Express 50p as a percentage of £2.

Solution

50p as a percentage of 200p is $\frac{50}{200} \times 100 = 25\%$

Percentage Change

To work out **percentage change**:

1. work out the change, e.g. increase, decrease, profit or loss
2. use the formula:

$$\text{Percentage change} = \frac{\text{change}}{\text{original amount}} \times 100\%$$

Example

Mr Smith bought a ring for £250 and sold it for £400. Work out his percentage profit.

Solution

$$\text{Percentage profit} = \frac{\text{profit}}{\text{original amount}} \times 100\%$$

£400 − £250 is £150 profit →

$$= \frac{150}{250} \times 100 = 60\%$$

Increasing or Decreasing Quantities by a Percentage

To increase or decrease a quantity by a percentage:
- work out the increase and add it on
- work out the decrease and subtract it.

Alternatively:
- write down the **multiplier**
- multiply the original amount by the multiplier.

Example

Increase £17 000 by 5%.

Solution A

5% of £17 000 is $\frac{5}{100} \times 17\,000 = £850$

New amount is £17 000 + £850 = £17 850

Solution B (Multiplier method)

5% extra is the same as 100% + 5% = 105%

105% is $\frac{105}{100} = 1.05$ ← The decimal equivalent is called the **multiplier**

105% of £17 000 is 1.05 × 17 000 = £17 850

Everyday Use of Percentages

Here are some examples of everyday use of percentages.

Example 1

I invest £500 at 3% simple interest for two years. How much interest do I earn?

Solution

Each year the interest earned is 3% of £500 $= \frac{3}{100} \times 500 = £15$

So the simple interest for two years is 2 × 15 = £30

Example 2

A builder quotes £350 + VAT for a job. VAT (Value Added Tax) is 20%. How much does the job cost altogether?

Solution

VAT is 20% of £350 $= \frac{20}{100} \times 350 = £70$

Or use a multiplier of 1.2

1.2 × 350 = £420

Total cost of job is £350 + £70 = £420

Example 3

Which offer is better value?

Offer 1

Offer 2

Solution

Problem Solving

When asked which is the 'better value' always work out the cost for the same quantity so that you can compare.

Offer 1 = 1000 g for £2.25

Offer 2 = 750 g for £1.80

Offer 1 would cost $\frac{£2.25}{4} = 56.25p$ for 250 g.

Offer 2 would cost $\frac{£1.80}{3} = 60p$ for 250 g.

Work out the cost of 250 g

So Offer 1 is better value.

Quick Test

1. a) Write $\frac{2}{5}$ as a decimal. b) Write 0.9 as a percentage. c) Write 35% as a fraction.
2. a) Work out 30% of 600 grams. b) Increase £14 by 20%.
3. The price of a car increases from £12 000 to £12 600. Work out the percentage increase.

Powers and Roots

Square and Cube Numbers

You need to know all the **square numbers** up to $15^2 = 225$

$1^2 =$	$2^2 =$	$3^2 =$	$4^2 =$	$5^2 =$	$6^2 =$	$7^2 =$	$8^2 =$
1	4	9	16	25	36	49	64

$9^2 =$	$10^2 =$	$11^2 =$	$12^2 =$	$13^2 =$	$14^2 =$	$15^2 =$
81	100	121	144	169	196	225

You need to know the following **cube numbers**:

$1^3 =$	$2^3 =$	$3^3 =$	$4^3 =$	$5^3 =$	$10^3 =$
1	8	27	64	125	1000

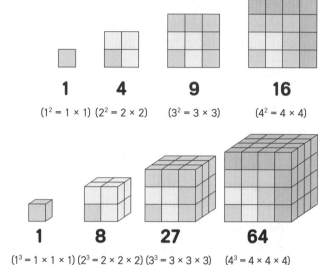

1 **4** **9** **16**
$(1^2 = 1 \times 1)$ $(2^2 = 2 \times 2)$ $(3^2 = 3 \times 3)$ $(4^2 = 4 \times 4)$

1 **8** **27** **64**
$(1^3 = 1 \times 1 \times 1)$ $(2^3 = 2 \times 2 \times 2)$ $(3^3 = 3 \times 3 \times 3)$ $(4^3 = 4 \times 4 \times 4)$

Square and Cube Roots

The **square root** of a given number is the number that multiplied by itself results in the given number.

For example, the square root of 25 is 5 because $5 \times 5 = 25$

$\sqrt{}$ is the symbol for square root so $\sqrt{25} = 5$

You need to know all these square roots:

$\sqrt{1} =$	$\sqrt{4} =$	$\sqrt{9} =$	$\sqrt{16} =$	$\sqrt{25} =$
1	2	3	4	5

$\sqrt{36} =$	$\sqrt{49} =$	$\sqrt{64} =$	$\sqrt{81} =$	$\sqrt{100} =$
6	7	8	9	10

$\sqrt{121} =$	$\sqrt{144} =$	$\sqrt{169} =$	$\sqrt{196} =$	$\sqrt{225} =$
11	12	13	14	15

The square root of a number can be positive or negative, e.g. $\sqrt{49} = +7$ or -7

The **cube root** of a given number is the number that multiplied by itself and by itself again results in the given number.

For example, the cube root of 64 is 4 because $4 \times 4 \times 4 = 64$

$\sqrt[3]{}$ is the symbol for cube root so $\sqrt[3]{64} = 4$

You need to know all these cube roots:

$\sqrt[3]{1} =$	$\sqrt[3]{8} =$	$\sqrt[3]{27} =$	$\sqrt[3]{64} =$	$\sqrt[3]{125} =$	$\sqrt[3]{1000} =$
1	2	3	4	5	10

Example

Between which two consecutive numbers does $\sqrt{70}$ lie?

Solution

Problem Solving

Find the nearest square roots that have a whole number answer. Remember consecutive numbers are next to each other.

$\sqrt{64} = 8$ and $\sqrt{81} = 9$

So $\sqrt{70}$ is between 8 and 9.

Square number • Cube number • Square root • Cube root

Working with Powers and Roots

The **power** or **index** (plural: indices) of a number is the number of times a number is multiplied by itself, e.g. $5^3 = 5 \times 5 \times 5$ and $2^4 = 2 \times 2 \times 2 \times 2$

When working with indices, follow these rules:
- To multiply powers of the same number, add the indices.
  $3^4 \times 3^5 = 3^{(4+5)} = 3^9$
- To divide powers of the same number, subtract the indices.
  $6^7 \div 6^2 = 6^{(7-2)} = 6^5$
- To work out the power of a number to another power, multiply the indices.
  $(10^2)^3 = 10^6$ (1 million)
- Any number to the power 1 is itself.
  $8^1 = 8$

Make sure that you know how to work with powers and roots on your calculator.

For example:

Input	Keys	Display
24^2	2 4 x^2 =	576
$\sqrt{289}$	$\sqrt{\blacksquare}$ 2 8 9 =	17
10^6	1 0 $x^\blacksquare$ 6 =	1 000 000
5^{-1}	5 x^{-1} =	0.2
$\sqrt[3]{90}$	SHIFT $\sqrt[3]{\blacksquare}$ 9 0 =	4.481…

Your calculator may work differently to the examples above. Make sure you know how it works.

Rules of indices also work in algebra. For example:
- $x^4 \times x^5 = x^{(4+5)} = x^9$
- $x^7 \div x^2 = x^{(7-2)} = x^5$
- $(x^2)^3 = x^6$

Example 1

a) Write $6^4 \times 6^5$ as a single power of 6.

Solution
$6^4 \times 6^5 = 6^{(4+5)} = 6^9$

b) Write $5^8 \div 5^4$ as a single power of 5.

Solution
$5^8 \div 5^4 = 5^{(8-4)} = 5^4$

c) Simplify $\frac{4^6 \times 4^2}{4^5}$

Solution
$\frac{4^6 \times 4^2}{4^5} = \frac{4^8}{4^5} = 4^3$

d) Simplify $\frac{3^8 \times 3^3}{3^7}$

Solution
$\frac{3^8 \times 3^3}{3^7} = \frac{3^{11}}{3^7}$
$= 3^4$

Example 2

Which is greater, 2^5 or 5^2?

Solution

Problem Solving
Use your knowledge of powers to work out the values and remember to say which is greater.

$2^5 = 2 \times 2 \times 2 \times 2 \times 2 = 32$
$5^2 = 25$

So 2^5 is greater.

Quick Test

1 Write down the value of:
a) 12^2 b) 3^3
c) $\sqrt{169}$ d) $\sqrt[3]{1000}$

2 Simplify:
a) $3^3 \times 3^5$ b) $8^6 \div 8^3$
c) $\frac{5^7 \times 5^3}{5^4}$

Ratio

Simplifying a Ratio

A **ratio** (:) is used to compare two or more quantities.

> ### Example 1
>
> Express 30 cm to 2 metres as a ratio in its simplest form.
>
> **Solution**
>
> 30 cm : 2 metres = 30 cm : 200 cm ←── When working with ratios, always use common units so they can cancel out
>
> = 3 : 20
>
> ### Example 2
>
> The scale on a map is given as 1 cm to 2 km. Express this as a ratio in its simplest form.
>
> **Solution**
>
> 1 km = 1000 metres; 1 metre = 100 cm
>
> So 2 km = 200 000 cm ←── Change to a common unit
>
> The ratio of the map is 1 cm : 200 000 cm
>
> = 1 : 200 000 ←── Cancel out the units
>
>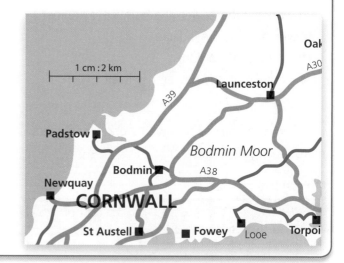

Ratios as Fractions

A ratio can be written as a fraction.

> ### Example
>
> Matthew and Natasha share a pizza in the ratio 3 : 2
>
> What fraction does Matthew eat?
>
> **Solution**
>
> | Problem Solving |
> | --- |
> | Use the total number of parts in the ratio to represent the total number of pieces of pizza. Then write the number Matthew eats as a fraction of the total number of pieces. |
>
> The ratio has 5 parts altogether.
>
> Matthew eats 3 out of the 5 pieces, so he eats $\frac{3}{5}$ of the pizza.
>
>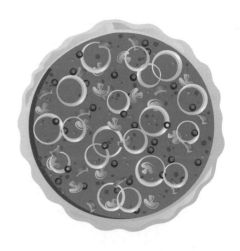

Dividing a Quantity in a Given Ratio

You can share quantities by using ratio. The parts in the ratio represent the proportions.

Example 1

An orange drink is made of orange juice and water in the ratio 1 : 4

How much water is used in a 200 ml drink?

Solution

There are 4 + 1 = 5 parts in the ratio altogether. So 5 parts is 200 ml.

1 part is 40 ml ← Dividing by 5

4 parts are 160 ml ← Multiplying by 4

So 160 ml of water is used.

Example 2

The ratio of adults to children at a football match is 7 : 3. There are 1500 children at the match. How many more adults are there than children?

Problem Solving

Always start by working out one part. Then work out how many more parts are for adults than children or work out the number of adults.

Solution A

Children represent 3 parts of the ratio.

So 3 parts = 1500

1 part = 500 ← Dividing by 3

Adults represent 4 more parts than children in the ratio.

So 4 parts = 2000 ← Multiplying by 4

There are 2000 more adults than children.

Solution B

Children represent 3 parts of the ratio.

So 3 parts = 1500

1 part = 500 ← Dividing by 3

Adults represent 7 parts.

So 7 parts = 3500 ← 500 × 7

3500 − 1500 = 2000 more adults than children

Quick Test

1. Write these ratios as simply as possible:
   a) 5 : 35   b) 66 : 44   c) 5 cm : 1 m   d) 2 kg : 400 g
2. $\frac{1}{3}$ of the students in a class are girls.
   a) Write the number of girls to the number of boys as a ratio.
   b) There are 18 boys. How many girls are there?
3. Divide £36 in the ratio 4 : 5
4. Work out the largest part if 180 kg is divided in the ratio 2 : 3 : 5

Proportion

Direct Proportion

Two values are in **direct proportion** if the ratio between them remains fixed as the values change.

Example 1

Two bags of flour cost £2.36
How much do three bags cost?

Solution
One bag costs $\frac{2.36}{2}$ = £1.18
So three bags cost 1.18 × 3 = £3.54

Example 2

Here is a recipe for Yorkshire pudding to serve four people:

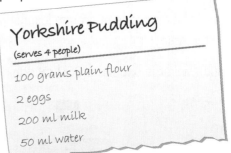

Yorkshire Pudding
(serves 4 people)

100 grams plain flour

2 eggs

200 ml milk

50 ml water

How much of each ingredient is needed to make Yorkshire pudding for six people?

Solution
6 people is
4 people + 2 people ← Half as many added on or one-and-a-half times as much

150 grams plain flour ← 100 g + 50 g or 1.5 × 100 g

3 eggs ← 2 eggs + 1 egg or 1.5 × 2 eggs

300 ml milk ←

75 ml water ← 200 ml + 100 ml or 1.5 × 200 ml

50 ml + 25 ml or 1.5 × 50 ml

Speed, Distance and Time

To measure **speed** you need to know the **distance** travelled and the **time** taken.

$$\text{Speed} = \frac{\text{distance}}{\text{time}}$$

The **units** for speed are usually one of:
- miles per hour (mph)
- kilometres per hour (km/h)
- metres per second (m/s).

At constant speed, distance is directly proportional to time.

Example

A car travels 150 metres in 10 seconds. How far will it travel in 30 seconds at the same speed?

Solution
The car will travel
15 metres in 1 second. ← Speed = 15 m/s

It will travel 15 × 30 ← Distance = speed × time
= 450 metres in 30 seconds.

Direct Proportion Graphs

If two quantities y and x are **directly proportional**, the graph will be a **straight line** through the origin.

This is the graph $y = 2x$ so every y-value is twice the corresponding x-value.

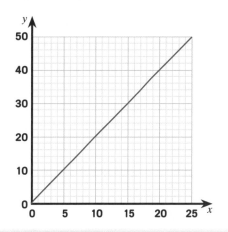

Exchange Rates

When you change money from one currency to another, you're given an **exchange rate**.

The exchange rate can vary for a number of reasons.

You will usually get a better rate when you buy a currency than when you sell the same currency.

Example

John is going on holiday to France. The exchange rate is £1 = €1.18

a) John changes £700 to euros. How many euros does he get?

Solution
£1 is worth €1.18
£700 is 700 × 1.18
= €826

If the rate is given as £1 = ..., then multiply when you leave the country

He gets €826.

b) At the end of the holiday John has €150 left.

He changes the euros back to pounds. The exchange rate is now £1 = €1.25

How many pounds does he get back?

Solution
€1.25 is worth £1.
So €150 is 150 ÷ 1.25
= £120

If the rate is given as £1 = ..., then divide when you come back

He gets back £120.

Quick Test

1. A car travels 90 miles in 1.5 hours. Work out the average speed.
2. £1 = $1.60
   a) Change £300 to dollars.   **b)** Change $500 to pounds.
3. £1 = €1.20
   a) Change £800 to euros.   **b)** Change €800 to pounds.

Key Words   Exchange rate

Basic Algebra

Algebra Facts

In **algebra** letters or symbols are used to represent numbers. The same rules work for algebra as work for arithmetic, but sometimes multiplication signs can be left out:

- $4 + a$ means 4 more than a
- $b - 5$ means 5 less than b
- $3c$ means $3 \times c$
- $\frac{d}{2}$ means $d \div 2$ or half of d
- ef means $e \times f$
- g^2 means $g \times g$

You need to know the meaning of these words:

- A **variable** is a letter that is used to represent any number, e.g. x or y.
- An **expression** is a combination of variables with numbers, e.g. $2x + 3y$ or $\frac{x}{2} + 1$
- An **equation** contains an equals sign and at least one variable, e.g. $2x + 5 = 16$ or $x + 3y = 7$
- A **formula** also contains an equals sign but is a rule connecting more than one variable, e.g. $A = \pi r^2$ or $s = \frac{d}{t}$
- A **term** is one part of an expression, equation or formula, e.g. $2x - 3y + 4$ has the three terms $2x$, $-3y$ and $+4$.
- An **integer** is a whole number.

A Formula in Words

You may be given a **formula in words**.

Example 1

Total pay = number of hours worked × pay per hour

Jack works for 35 hours and is paid £9.50 per hour.

Work out his total pay.

Solution

Total pay = number of hours worked × pay per hour

So total pay is 35 × 9.50 = £332.50

Example 2

Use this formula to work out the number of litres of petrol used on a journey of 90 miles:

Petrol used (litres) = number of miles ÷ 12

Solution

Petrol used (litres) = 90 ÷ 12

= 7.5 litres

Collecting Like Terms

Like terms are terms with the same variable, e.g. $2x$ and $3x$; $2xy$ and $3xy$; x^2 and $4x^2$

To **simplify** an expression, you **collect like terms**.

Example

a) Simplify $3x + 4x$

Solution

$3x + 4x$ simplifies to $7x$

b) Simplify fully $x^2 + 4x - 7x + 3x^2$

Solution

$x^2 + 4x - 7x + 3x^2$
simplifies to $4x^2 - 3x$

$x^2 + 3x^2 = 4x^2$ and $+4x - 7x = -3x$

c) Simplify $xy + 3yx - 2xy$

Solution

$xy + 3yx - 2xy$
simplifies to $2xy$

Note that yx is the same as xy

Key Words Algebra • Variable • Expression • Equation • Formula • Term • Integer • Like terms • Simplify

Substitution

Substitution is replacing variables (letters) with numbers.

Example 1

If $x = 2$, $y = -3$ and $z = 0$, work out the value of:

a) $5x - 4y$

Solution

$5x - 4y = 5 \times 2 - 4 \times -3$ ← Substitute the values for x and y

$= 10 + 12 = 22$ ← Show your working out

b) xyz

Solution

$xyz = 2 \times -3 \times 0 = 0$ ← Substitute the values for x, y and z

c) $y^2 - x$

Solution

$y^2 - x = (-3)^2 - 2$ ← Use brackets as the minus sign is also squared

$= 9 - 2 = 7$ ← Show your working out

Example 2

You are given that n is a positive integer.

Show clearly why $2n + 1$ is always odd.

Solution

Problem Solving

It's not enough to simply substitute values for n. This would only show it's true for those particular values.

An integer is a whole number.

$2 \times$ any positive whole number is always even. ← Multiples of 2 are even

Even $+ 1 =$ odd

So $2n + 1$ is always odd.

Changing the Subject of a Formula

To **change the subject** of a formula:

1 collect all subject terms to one side of the formula

2 collect everything else to the other side

3 rearrange to leave the subject on its own.

Example 1

Make x the subject of $y = 3x + 2$

Solution

$y - 2 = 3x$ ← Collect the subject term ($3x$) to one side and everything else to the other by subtracting 2 from both sides

$\dfrac{y - 2}{3} = x$ ← Divide by 3 to leave the subject (x) on its own

Example 2

Make r the subject of $C = 2\pi r$

Solution

$\dfrac{C}{2\pi} = r$ ← Dividing both sides by 2π to leave the subject (r) on its own

Quick Test

1 An approximate rule to change Celsius (°C) to Fahrenheit (°F) is 'double the Celsius temperature and add 30'. Use this rule to change 10°C to °F.

2 Simplify:
  a) $8x - 3x$
  b) $2x + 3y - 6x + 4y$
  c) $4x^2 + 5xy - 6x^2 + 4xy$
  d) $5x + 4y + 2x - 4y + z - 2z$

3 You are given that $x = 4$, $y = -\frac{1}{2}$ and $z = -1$. Work out the value of:
  a) $2x + 6y$
  b) $3x + y - 4z$
  c) $xy - yz$

4 Make x the subject of:
  a) $y = 5x - 4$
  b) $y = 3(x + 2)$

Key Words   Substitution • Change the subject   25

Working with Brackets & Trial and Improvement

Multiplying Out Brackets

To **expand** or **multiply out** brackets every term in the bracket is multiplied by the term outside the bracket.

Example

a) Multiply out $5(x + 4)$

Solution
$5(x + 4) = 5x + 20$

b) Multiply out $y(y - 6)$

Solution
$y(y - 6) = y^2 - 6y$

c) Expand and simplify $9(x - 3) - 2(3x - 4)$

Solution
$9(x - 3) - 2(3x - 4)$

> Multiply out each bracket separately. Remember $-2 \times -4 = +8$

$= 9x - 27 - 6x + 8$

$= 3x - 19$

> Collect like terms

d) Expand $4t^2(2t + s)$

Solution
$4t^2(2t + s) = 8t^3 + 4t^2s$

Factorisation

Factorisation is the reverse process of multiplying out brackets. To factorise, you have to look for common factors in every term.

Example

Factorise:

a) $3x + 6$

Solution
$3x + 6 = 3(x + 2)$

> 3 is the common factor of $3x$ and 6

b) $4x^2 + 3x$

Solution
$4x^2 + 3x = x(4x + 3)$

> x is the highest common factor of $4x^2$ and $3x$

c) $8xy - 6x^2$

Solution
$8xy - 6x^2 = 2x(4y - 3x)$

> $2x$ is the highest common factor of $8xy$ and $-6x^2$

Key Words　　　　**Expand • Multiply out • Factorisation**

Working with Brackets & Trial and Improvement

Trial and Improvement

Trial and improvement can be used to find approximate solutions to **equations** (see page 28 for more about equations). A solution is a value that works for the equation.

Trial and improvement involves trying values and improving them to get as close as possible to the solution.

Example 1

Use trial and improvement to find the solution to $x^3 = 30$. Give your answer to 1 decimal place.

Solution

x	x^3	Comment
3	27	Too small
4	64	Too big
3.2	32.768	Too big
3.1	29.791	Too small
3.15	31.255 875	Too big

Solution between $x = 3$ and $x = 4$

Solution between $x = 3.1$ and $x = 3.2$

The solution is between $x = 3.1$ and $x = 3.15$
So to 1 decimal place, the solution is $x = 3.1$

Example 2

Show that the equation $x^3 - 12x = 50$ has a solution between 4 and 5.

Solution

> **Problem Solving**
> Write the equation with all terms on one side, then complete a table to present your answer clearly and logically.

$x^3 - 12x - 50 = 0$

x	$x^3 - 12x - 50$	Comment
4	$4^3 - (12 \times 4) - 50 = -34$	Too small
5	$5^3 - (12 \times 5) - 50 = 15$	Too big

So the solution is between 4 and 5.

Example 3

Find the two consecutive whole numbers between which the solution of $x^3 + 2x = 60$ lies.

Solution

> **Problem Solving**
> Set up a table as normal and then try whole numbers. Remember that consecutive numbers are next to each other.

$x^3 + 2x - 60 = 0$

x	$x^3 + 2x - 60$	Comment
2	$2^3 + (2 \times 2) - 60 = -48$	Too small
3	$3^3 + (2 \times 3) - 60 = -27$	Too small
4	$4^3 + (2 \times 4) - 60 = 12$	Too big

So the solution is between 3 and 4.

Quick Test

1. Multiply out:
   a) $5(2x + 3)$
   b) $3(4x - 2y)$
   c) $x(x - 7)$
   d) $2x(x + 2y - 3z)$
2. Factorise:
   a) $3x + 6$
   b) $4x + 10y$
   c) $8x^2 - 12x$
   d) $15xy - 10x^2$
3. Use trial and improvement to find a solution to 1 decimal place.
   a) $x^3 = 20$
   b) $x^3 - 10x + 6 = 0$
   c) $x^3 - 8x + 1 = 0$

Linear Equations

Equations

An **equation** has an unknown value to be worked out. This is called **solving** the equation.

The simplest equations are those with only one step.

Example

Solve:

a) $x + 4 = 7$ **Solution** $x = 3$ ← Subtract 4 from both sides

b) $x - 5 = 11$ **Solution** $x = 16$

c) $2x = 8$ **Solution** $x = 4$

d) $\dfrac{x}{10} = 3$ **Solution** $x = 30$ ← Multiply both sides by 10

Using the Balance Method to Solve Equations

The sides of an equation should **balance**.
So whatever you do to one side of the equation you must also do to the other side.

Example 1

Solve $2x + 3 = 11$

Solution

$$2x \;+\; 3 = 11$$
$$-\;3 \qquad -\;3$$
$$2x = 8$$
$$\frac{2x}{2} = \frac{8}{2}$$
$$x = 4$$

Subtract 3 from both sides of the equation to leave just the x-term on the left-hand side. Note that +3 and −3 give a zero, shown by the circle

Divide both sides by 2 to leave just x on the left-hand side

Example 2

Solve $8x - 5 = 4x + 3$

Solution

$$8x \;-\; 5 = 4x \;+\; 3$$
$$+\;5 \qquad\quad +\;5$$
$$8x = 4x + 8$$
$$-\;4x \qquad -\;4x$$
$$4x = 8$$
$$\frac{4x}{4} = \frac{8}{4}$$
$$x = 2$$

Add 5 to both sides of the equation to leave just the x-term on the left-hand side. Note that −5 and +5 give a zero, shown by the circle

Subtract $4x$ from both sides of the equation to leave just the number 8 on the right-hand side. Note that $4x$ and $-4x$ give a zero, shown by the circle

Divide both sides by 4 to leave just x on the left-hand side

Example 3

Solve $6(2x - 1) = 10x + 20$

Solution

$$12x - 6 = 10x + 20$$ ← Multiply out the brackets

$$12x \boxed{- 6} = 10x + 20$$
$$\boxed{+ 6} \qquad\quad + 6$$

← Add 6 to both sides of the equation to leave just the x-term on the left-hand side. Note that −6 and +6 give a zero, shown by the circle

$$12x = \boxed{10x} + 26$$
$$-10x \quad \boxed{-10x}$$

← Subtract 10x from both sides of the equation to leave just the number 26 on the right-hand side. Note that 10x and −10x give a zero, shown by the circle

$$2x = 26$$

$$\frac{2x}{2} = \frac{26}{2}$$ ← Divide both sides by 2 to leave just x on the left-hand side

$$x = 13$$

Example 4

The sum of x, $4x$ and $x + 1$ is 43.

Work out the value of x.

Solution

Problem Solving

Always set up an equation to work out the answer. If you use trial and improvement, you may not find the answer. Once you have set up the equation, solve it as normal.

$$x + 4x + x + 1 = 43$$

$$6x \boxed{+ 1} = 43$$
$$\boxed{- 1} \quad - 1$$

← Subtract 1 from both sides of the equation to leave just the x-term on the left-hand side

$$6x = 42$$

$$\frac{6x}{6} = \frac{42}{6}$$ ← Divide both sides by 6 to leave just x on the left-hand side

$$x = 7$$

Quick Test

Solve these equations:

1. a) $5x = 20$ b) $x + 9 = 12$ c) $x - 2 = 8$ d) $\frac{x}{5} = 3$
2. a) $5x - 7 = 8$ b) $7x - 1 = 13$ c) $6x + 5 = 2x$ d) $4x + 1 = x - 8$
3. a) $3x + 5 = x - 9$ b) $8x - 1 = 3x + 9$ c) $5x + 1 = 3x + 7$ d) $\frac{1}{2}x - 2 = 7 - x$
4. a) $6(2x + 1) = 30$ b) $3(2x - 5) = 9$ c) $8(x - 1) = 48$ d) $3(x + 1) = x + 4$

Patterns and Sequences

Important Number Sequences

You should be familiar with these number sequences:

- **Odd** numbers:

  1   3   5   7   9   ...

- **Even** numbers:

  2   4   6   8   10   ...

- **Square** numbers:

  1   4   9   16   25   ...

- **Cube** numbers:

  1   8   27   64   125   ...

Patterns and Sequences

These shapes follow a pattern.

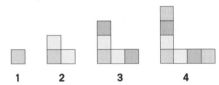

You may be asked to:

- draw the next shape in a pattern
- work out the rule for continuing a pattern
- use the rule to solve problems.

You can use a table.

Shape Number	1	2	3	4
No. of Squares	1	3	5	7

In this example the number of squares increases by 2 each time, so shape 5 will have 9 squares.

You also need to know the following:

- A **sequence** is a set of numbers with a rule to find each number.
- A **term-to-term rule** is a rule that links one term to the next term, e.g. the term-to-term rule for odd numbers is 'add 2'.
- A **position-to-term rule** is a rule that links the position of the term to the term, e.g. the position-to-term rule for odd numbers is 'double the position number and subtract 1':

Position	1	2	3	4	5
Term	1	3	5	7	9

So the 5th term is $2 \times 5 - 1 = 9$

The nth Term of a Sequence

The nth term of a sequence is a formula for the position-to-term rule, e.g. the formula for the nth term for odd numbers would be $2n - 1$.

So sequences that go up in 2s are of the form $2n + c$ and sequences that go up in 3s are of the form $3n + c$, and so on.

N.B. A common mistake is to give the term-to-term rule as the nth term.

Example 1

Work out the nth term of this sequence:

7   10   13   16   19   ...

Solution

The term-to-term rule is 'add 3':

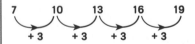

This means the sequence is linked to the 3 times table.

So the nth term will be of the form $3n + c$.

When $n = 1$: $3 \times 1 + c = 7$, so $c = 4$

So the nth term is $3n + 4$.

Key Words   Sequence • Term-to-term rule • Position-to-term rule

Example 2

Work out the nth term of this sequence:

11   9   7   5 ...

Solution

The term-to-term rule is 'subtract 2':

This means the sequence is linked to the 2 times table.

So the nth term will be of the form $-2n + c$.

When $n = 1$: $-2 \times 1 + c = 11$, so $c = 13$

So the nth term is $-2n + 13$ or $13 - 2n$.

Example 3

A café has tables to seat 4 people. When put together 2 tables can seat 6 people, and so on.

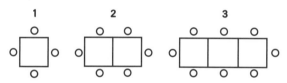

a) How many people can sit at 4 tables put together in this way?

Solution

Position	1	2	3
Term	4	6	8

The term-to-term rule is 'add 2'.

So the number of people that can sit at 4 tables is $8 + 2 = 10$

b) How many people can sit at n tables put together in this way?

Solution

The nth term will be of the form $2n + c$.

When $n = 1$: $2 \times 1 + c = 4$, so $c = 2$

So the nth term is $2n + 2$.

Example 4

Jack says that 87 is in this sequence:

6   13   20 27 34 ...

Is he correct? You must show your working.

Solution

Problem Solving
To test if a number is part of a sequence, work out the nth term and test if an integer value for n gives that number.

The term-to-term rule is 'add 7':

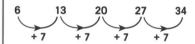

So the nth term will be of the form $7n + c$.

When $n = 1$: $7 \times 1 + c = 6$, so $c = -1$

So the nth term is $7n - 1$.

If 87 is in the sequence, $7n - 1 = 87$ will give a whole number solution.

$7n = 88$, so $n = 12.57$. This means that 87 is between the 12th and 13th terms.

> The 12th term is $7 \times 12 - 1 = 83$ and the 13th term is $7 \times 13 - 1 = 90$

Jack isn't correct.

Quick Test

1 Here is a pattern made of matchsticks:

  a) Draw the next pattern.

  b) How many sticks are used to make the 10th pattern?

  c) What is the biggest pattern that can be made using 50 sticks?

2 For each sequence:

  i) write down the next two terms

  ii) work out the nth term

  iii) work out the 20th term.

  a) 5   8   11   14   17 ...

  b) 10 14 18 22 26 ...

Straight Line Graphs

Linear Graphs

A **linear graph** is a straight line graph, e.g. $y = x$, $y = 2x + 3$, $x + y = 5$, etc.

To draw the graph:

1 choose three values for x (pick any three easy values in the range of the graph – the highest and lowest are often sensible points to use)

2 work out the corresponding y-values

3 plot the points on a grid

4 draw a straight, ruled line through the points.

Sometimes you will be given a table of values to complete.

Example 1

a) Complete the table of values for $y = 2x + 3$

x	−2	−1	0	1	2
y	−1				7

Solution

When $x = -1$, $y = 2 \times -1 + 3 = 1$ ◀ Work out each corresponding y-value

When $x = 0$, $y = 2 \times 0 + 3 = 3$

When $x = 1$, $y = 2 \times 1 + 3 = 5$

x	−2	−1	0	1	2
y	−1	1	3	5	7

This gives the points to plot on the grid: (−2, −1), (−1, 1), (0, 3), (1, 5) and (2, 7)

b) Draw the graph of $y = 2x + 3$ for values of x from −2 to 2.

Solution

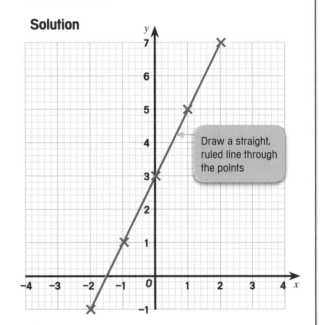

Draw a straight, ruled line through the points

Example 2

Draw the graph of $x + y = 5$ for values of x from 0 to 5.

Solution

Choosing $x = 0$, $x = 2$ and $x = 5$ ◀ Choose three values for x

When $x = 0$, $y = 5$

When $x = 2$, $y = 3$ ◀ Work out each corresponding y-value

When $x = 5$, $y = 0$

x	0	2	5
y	5	3	0

This gives the points to plot on the grid: (0, 5), (2, 3) and (5, 0)

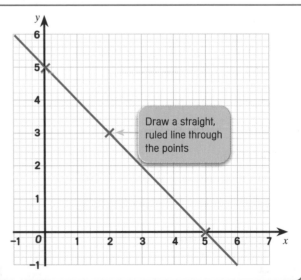

Draw a straight, ruled line through the points

Gradient

Gradient is a measure of the amount a line slopes.
To work out the gradient of a straight line:
1. choose two points on the line and join them
2. draw a right-angled triangle using the line already drawn as the hypotenuse
3. use the formula shown opposite.

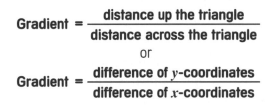

$$\text{Gradient} = \frac{\text{distance up the triangle}}{\text{distance across the triangle}}$$

or

$$\text{Gradient} = \frac{\text{difference of } y\text{-coordinates}}{\text{difference of } x\text{-coordinates}}$$

Remember the following about lines and their gradients:
- A line sloping up from left to right has a **positive** gradient.
- A line sloping down from left to right has a **negative** gradient.

Example

Work out the gradient of these straight lines.

a)

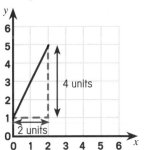

Solution

Gradient is:

$$\frac{\text{distance up the triangle}}{\text{distance across the triangle}} = \frac{4}{2} = 2$$

b)

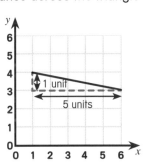

Negative gradient as the line slopes down from left to right

Solution

Gradient is:

$$\frac{\text{distance up the triangle}}{\text{distance across the triangle}} = -\frac{1}{5}$$

Quick Test

1. Draw the graph of $y = 2x - 3$ for values of x from 0 to 4.
2. Draw the graph of $x + y = 4$ for values of x from 0 to 4.
3. Draw the graph of $y = 3x - 1$ for values of x from −1 to 3.
4. Work out the gradient of the line shown.

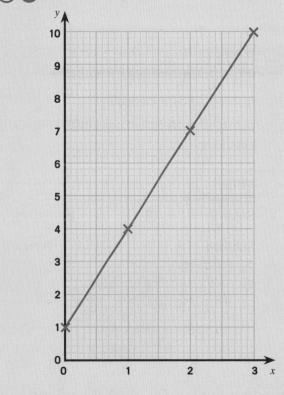

Linear Inequalities and Quadratic Graphs

Inequalities on a Number Line

Inequalities use the symbols:

- $<$ to mean 'less than'
- $>$ to mean 'greater than'
- $\leqslant$ to mean 'less than or equal to'
- $\geqslant$ to mean 'greater than or equal to'.

The solution to an inequality can be shown on a **number line** using open circles (O) and closed circles (●):

 means $x <$  means $x \leqslant$

○—→ means $x >$　　●—→ means $x \geqslant$

Example

Show each of these inequalities on a number line.

a) $x < 1$

Solution

b) $x > 4$

Solution

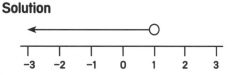

c) $x \leqslant 1$

Solution

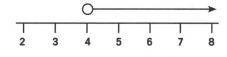

d) $x \geqslant 4$

Solution

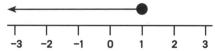

e) $-2 \leqslant x < 5$

Solution

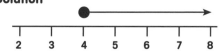

Solving Linear Inequalities

When solving a **linear inequality**:

- use the same techniques as when solving an equation

- always collect terms so that the x-term has a positive coefficient
- never replace the inequality symbol with an equals sign.

Example

a) Solve $2x + 1 < 19$

Solution

$2x + 1 < 19$

$2x < 18$ ← Subtract 1 from both sides

$x < 9$ ← Divide both sides by 2

b) Solve $3x - 3 \geqslant x + 7$

Solution

$3x - 3 \geqslant x + 7$

$2x - 3 \geqslant 7$ ← Subtract x from both sides

$2x \geqslant 10$ ← Add 3 to both sides

$x \geqslant 5$ ← Divide both sides by 2

c) Work out the integers that satisfy $6 < 3x \leqslant 12$

Solution

$6 < 3x \leqslant 12$

$2 < x \leqslant 4$ ← Divide through by 3

3 and 4 satisfy the inequality.

Integers are the whole numbers that satisfy the inequality

Linear Inequalities and Quadratic Graphs

Quadratic Graphs

A **quadratic graph** is a curved graph $\cup$ or $\cap$.

To draw a quadratic graph:
1. complete a table of values
2. plot the points and draw a smooth curve.

Example 1

Draw the graph of $y = x^2$ for values of x from -3 to 3.

Solution

x	-3	-2	-1	0	1	2	3
y	9	4	1	0	1	4	9

$y = x^2$

Plot the points $(-3, 9)$, $(-2, 4)$ and so on

Draw a smooth curve through the points

Example 2

a) Draw the graph of $y = 2x^2 - x - 3$ for values of x from -1 to 2.

Solution

x	-1	0	1	2
$2x^2$	2	0	2	8
$-x$	1	0	-1	-2
-3	-3	-3	-3	-3
y	0	-3	-2	3

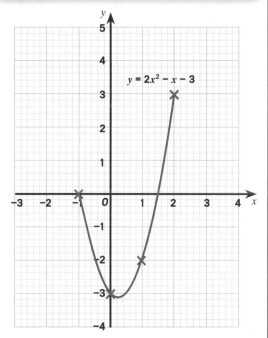

$y = 2x^2 - x - 3$

b) Use the graph to solve $2x^2 - x - 3 = 0$

Solution

$x = -1$ and $x = 1.5$ ← Read off at the points where $y = 0$ intersects the curve

Quick Test

1. Show each of the following inequalities on a number line.
   a) $x \leqslant 3$ **b)** $x > 2$ **c)** $0 < x \leqslant 4$
2. Solve these inequalities:
   a) $2x - 8 > 0$ **b)** $5x - 4 \leqslant 2x + 5$ **c)** $2(x + 3) \geqslant 9$
3. Draw the graph of $y = x^2 - 2x - 2$ for values of x from -2 to 4.

Real-life Graphs

Functional Graphs

Functional graphs:
- can be used to solve a real-life problem
- are often straight line graphs but may also be curved.

Example 1

A plumber has a call-out charge of £30. He then charges £25 per hour for each job.

a) Show these charges on a graph.

Solution

Graph must pass through (0, 30) – call-out charge even if no work is done – and (1, 55)

For each hour the cost increases by £25 so for a job taking 2 hours the charge is £80

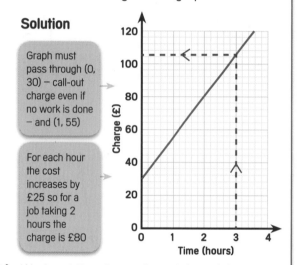

b) Work out the charge for a 3-hour job.

Solution

Reading from the graph the charge is £105.

Check: 30 + (3 × 25) = £105 ✔

Example 2

The graph shows the value of a car with age.

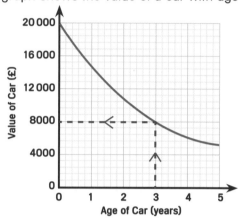

Show that after 3 years the car is only worth 40% of its value when new.

Solution

Problem Solving
Use the graph to get the price of the car when new and then work out 40% of that value. Check your calculation by reading from the graph at 3 years.

Value when new = £20 000

40% of £20 000 is $\frac{40}{100}$ × 20 000 = £8000

Reading at 3 years on the graph gives £8000, so the car is only worth 40% of its original value.

Conversion Graphs

A **conversion graph** is used to convert from one unit to another and back again.

Example

a) Given that 8 gallons = 36 litres, draw a conversion graph.

Solution

The conversion graph will be a straight line through (0, 0) and (8, 36)

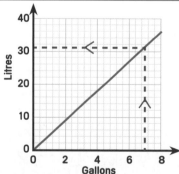

b) Convert 7 gallons to litres.

Solution

Reading from the graph 7 gallons is approximately 31.5 litres.

Conversion graph

Travel Graphs

You can use a **travel graph** (also called a **distance–time graph**) to:

- read information such as the distance travelled after a given time
- work out the average speed of a journey

> **Average speed = $\dfrac{\text{distance travelled}}{\text{time taken}}$**

- decide which part of a journey is faster.

The **steeper** a line is on the graph, the **faster** the journey. A **horizontal line** means there is **no movement** (the journey has stopped).

Example

The graph shows a journey of a delivery driver.

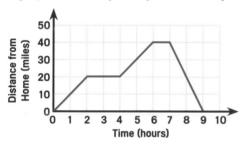

a) How many times does the delivery driver stop during the journey? Explain your answer.

Solution

The driver stops twice as there are two parts of the graph with horizontal lines.

b) How far does she travel altogether?

Solution

She travels 40 miles each way so
40 × 2 = 80 miles

c) Work out the average speed for the first part of the journey.

Solution

Average speed = $\dfrac{\text{distance travelled}}{\text{time taken}}$

$= \dfrac{20}{2} = 10$ mph

Quick Test

1. A taxi driver has a £4 minimum charge for up to 2 miles. He then charges 50p for every extra half a mile.
   a) Show this information on graph paper.
   b) How much would a 5-mile journey cost?

2. Use the graph below to convert:
   a) £150 to dollars ($)
   b) $400 to pounds (£).

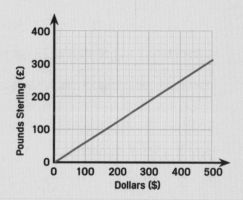

3. The graph shows a journey from O to C.

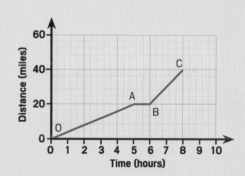

   a) Which part of the journey is the fastest? Give a reason for your answer.
   b) How far is C from O?
   c) What is happening between 5 hours and 6 hours?
   d) Work out the average speed for the whole journey.

Exam Practice Questions

You may wish to answer these questions on a separate piece of paper so that you can show full working out, which you will be expected to do in the exam.

Questions labelled with an asterisk (*) are ones where the quality of your written communication (QWC) will be assessed.

1. **a)** Write the number two thousand and eighteen in digits. **(1)**

  b) Write the number 1070 in words. **(1)**

  c) Write the number 387 to the nearest 10. **(1)**

2. There are 62 seats in a train carriage. 58 passengers are in the carriage.

  At the station 14 get off and 27 get on.

  How many passengers will have to stand up if all the seats are now taken? **(3)**

3. Here is a list of numbers:

  6   9   13   15   18   20   27

  From the list:

  a) write down the square number. **(1)**

  b) write down the prime number. **(1)**

  c) write down the cube number. **(1)**

4. Here is a pattern made from matchsticks:

1   2   3

a) Draw the next pattern on a separate piece of paper. **(1)**

b) Work out the number of sticks in pattern 10. **(2)**

c) Andrew says there is a pattern with 84 sticks in it.

Explain why he must be wrong. **(1)**

5. a) Simplify $x + 2x + 4x$ **(1)**

b) Work out the value of $3x + 5y$ when $x = 8$ and $y = -4$ **(2)**

6. a) Solve $\frac{x}{5} = 10$ **(1)**

b) Solve $3x - 2 = 16$ **(2)**

c) Solve $4(2x + 5) = -28$ **(3)**

7. Here is a coordinate grid:

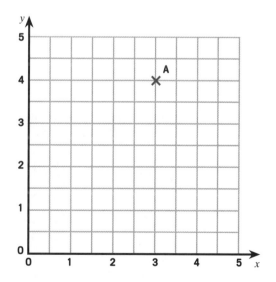

a) Write down the coordinates of A. (............ , ...) **(1)**

b) Plot the point (1, 1) on the grid. Label it B. **(1)**

c) Write down the coordinates of the midpoint of AB. (............ , ...) **(2)**

8. **a)** Complete the table of values for $y = 3x - 4$ (2)

x	−1	0	1	2	3
y	−7		−1		5

b) On the grid draw the graph of $y = 3x - 4$ for values of x from −1 to 3. (2)

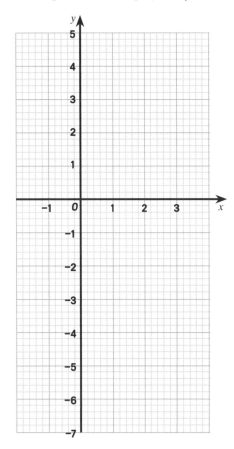

*9. Matt wants a new fridge. Three shops have these adverts for the fridge he wants.

FRIDGE WORLD

$\frac{1}{3}$ off usual price of **£480**

FRIDGE BARGAINS

■■ PAY DEPOSIT OF £40 ■■

Then pay 12 equal instalments of £25

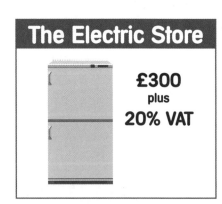

The Electric Store

£300 plus **20% VAT**

Matt wants to pay as little as possible.

From which shop should he buy the fridge? Show clearly how you get your answer.   **(6)**

10. The nth term of a sequence is $5n + 3$.

   a) Find the sixth term of the sequence.   **(2)**

   b) Is the number 47 a term in the sequence? Give reasons for your answer.   **(2)**

11. Mr Smith bought a new car for £16 500 in January 2008. He sold it for £6900 in January 2011.

   Annual depreciation = $\dfrac{\text{original price (£)} - \text{selling price (£)}}{\text{number of years}}$

   a) Use the formula to work out the annual depreciation of the car.   **(2)**

   b) Estimate the value of the car in January 2012.   **(2)**

12. **a)** Express 42 as a product of prime factors.   **(2)**

   b) Express 42^2 as a product of prime factors.   **(1)**

13. Harry earned £15 000 last year. He does not pay tax on the first £5040.

   Kim earned £14 400 last year. She does not pay tax on the first £8100.

   They both pay tax on 20% of the rest of their earnings.

   *a) Who pays the most tax and by how much?   **(4)**

   *b) Who takes home the most pay and by how much?   **(2)**

Symmetry and Shapes

Line Symmetry

A **line of symmetry** is sometimes called a **mirror line**. It reflects one half of a shape onto the other half of the shape.

You will need to:
- draw lines of symmetry on a 2-D shape
- recognise shapes that have line symmetry
- work out how many lines of symmetry a shape has.

N.B. You can sometimes use your calculator screen as a mirror to check whether your line is correct.

Example 1

Draw all the lines of symmetry on these letters:

A C F H

Solution

One line of symmetry	One line of symmetry	No lines of symmetry	Two lines of symmetry

Example 2

Reflect the shaded shape in the mirror line.

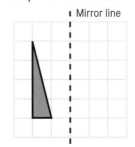

Solution

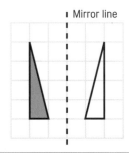

Rotational Symmetry

The **order of rotational symmetry** is the number of times a shape looks the same as it moves through one complete turn.

You will need to:
- find the order of rotational symmetry of a 2-D shape
- recognise shapes that have rotational symmetry.

N.B. You can use tracing paper to help you count the number of times a shape looks the same as the original when rotated.

Example 1

Write down the order of rotational symmetry for each of these letters:

M N X P

Solution

   P

Order 1 (no rotational symmetry)	Order 2	Order 4	Order 1

Example 2

Shade two more squares so that the shape has rotational symmetry of order 2.

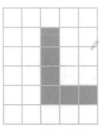

Solution

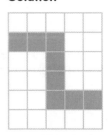

Triangles

There are four types of **triangle**:

- A **right-angled triangle** has an angle of 90°.
- An **equilateral triangle** has three equal sides and three equal angles.
- An **isosceles triangle** has two equal sides and two equal angles.
- A **scalene triangle** has no equal sides and no equal angles.

An equilateral triangle has **three lines of symmetry** and **rotational symmetry of order 3**.

An isosceles triangle has **one line of symmetry**.

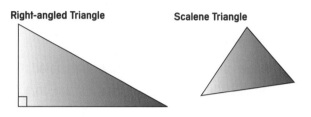

Right-angled Triangle

Scalene Triangle

Equilateral Triangle

Isosceles Triangle

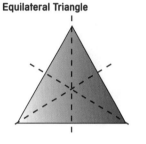

Quadrilaterals

A **quadrilateral** is any four-sided shape.

There are several types of quadrilateral:

- A **square** has four equal sides and four right angles.
- A **rectangle** has equal opposite sides and four right angles.
- A **parallelogram** has equal opposite sides and equal opposite angles.
- A **rhombus** has four equal sides and equal opposite angles.
- A **kite** has two pairs of equal adjacent sides.
- A **trapezium** has one pair of parallel sides:

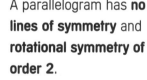

A square has **four lines of symmetry** and **rotational symmetry of order 4**.

A rectangle has **two lines of symmetry** and **rotational symmetry of order 2**.

A parallelogram has **no lines of symmetry** and **rotational symmetry of order 2**.

A rhombus has **two lines of symmetry** and **rotational symmetry of order 2**.

A kite has **one line of symetry** and **no rotational symmetry**.

Quick Test

1. For these letters write down:
   a) the number of lines of symmetry
   b) the order of rotational symmetry.
   E I Z B S T V W

Congruency, Similarity and 3-D Shapes

Congruent Shapes

Two shapes are **congruent** if they're the **same size** and the **same shape**.

When shapes are reflected, rotated or translated (see page 62), the image is congruent to the object.

All these shapes are congruent:

Example

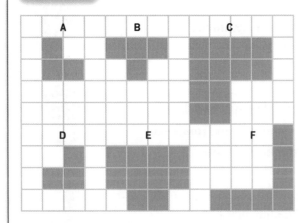

a) Which **two** shapes are congruent to shape A?

Solution

Shapes C and E are congruent to shape A.

b) Name **two** other shapes that are congruent.

Solution

Shapes D and F are a pair of congruent shapes.

Similar Shapes

Two shapes are **similar** if one shape is an enlargement of the other:

- The angles in one shape will be equal to the corresponding angles in the other shape.
- The corresponding sides of each shape are in the same ratio.

These triangles are similar:

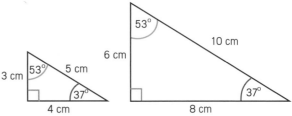

Example

a) Which shape is similar to shape A?

Solution

Shape C is similar to shape A because all lengths have been doubled.

Note that the area of shape C is four times the area of shape A

b) Explain why shape F isn't similar to shape A.

Solution

To be similar, all lengths have to be multiplied by the same number (scale factor). Some of the lengths have doubled but others have stayed the same.

3-D Shapes

You need to be able to recognise and draw these shapes:

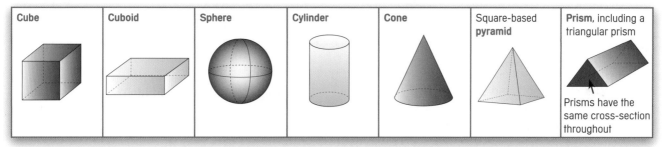

Cube	Cuboid	Sphere	Cylinder	Cone	Square-based pyramid	Prism, including a triangular prism

Prisms have the same cross-section throughout

Cubes and cuboids can be drawn on **isometric** paper. Some prisms can also be drawn on isometric paper.

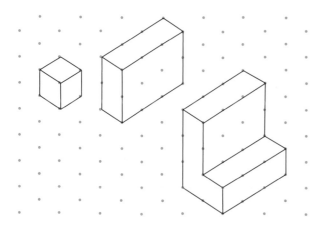

Faces, Edges and Vertices

Here is a cuboid:

A cuboid has:

- 6 **faces**
- 12 **edges**
- 8 **vertices**.

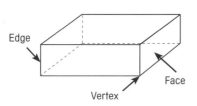

Edge

Face

Vertex

Example

Here is a triangular prism. How many faces, edges and vertices does it have?

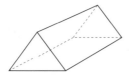

Solution

There are 5 faces, 9 edges and 6 vertices.

Don't forget to count faces, edges and vertices that you can't see

Quick Test

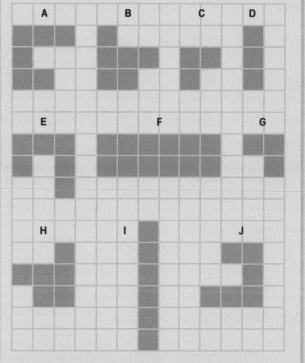

1. Complete the sentences.
   a) Shape A is congruent to shape _____ and shape _____.
   b) Shape B is congruent to shape _____.
   c) Shape C is congruent to shape _____.
   d) Shape D is similar to shape _____.

2. How many faces, edges and vertices does a square-based pyramid have?

Key Words   Cube • Cuboid • Sphere • Cylinder • Cone • Pyramid • Prism • Face • Edge • Vertex

Angles and Parallel Lines

Angle Facts

Acute angles are less than 90°.

Obtuse angles are between 90° and 180°.

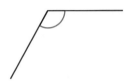

Reflex angles are between 180° and 360°.

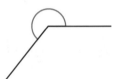

Angles **on a straight line** add up to 180°.

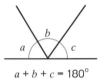

$$a + b + c = 180°$$

Angles **at a point** add up to 360°.

$$a + b + c + d = 360°$$

Vertically opposite angles are **equal**.

$$a = b$$
$$c = d$$

Parallel Lines

Alternate angles are equal.

Corresponding angles are equal.

 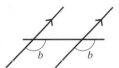

Allied angles add up to 180°.

$$c + d = 180°$$

Key Words   Acute angle • Obtuse angle • Reflex angle • Alternate angles • Corresponding angles

Example 1

Work out the value of x.

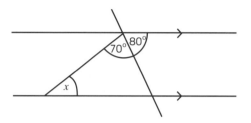

Problem Solving

Because there are parallel lines, look out for any alternate or corresponding angles.

Solution A

Filling in the missing angle on the straight line gives 30°.

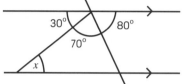

x and 30° are alternate angles, so $x = 30°$

Solution B

The other angle in the triangle and 80° are alternate angles.

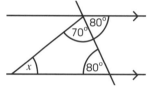

Angles in a triangle add up to 180°, so x is $180° - 70° - 80° = 30°$

Example 2

Show that AC is parallel to DG.

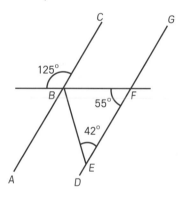

Solution

Problem Solving

Mark any missing angles you know on the diagram.

Angle CBF is $180° - 125° = 55°$ ← Angles on a straight line

Angle CBF = angle BFE, so they are alternate angles on parallel lines AC and DG.

N.B. You don't use the angle of 42° to answer the question.

Quick Test

 1 In each part, work out the value of x.
Give reasons for your answers.

a)

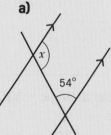

b)

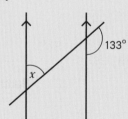

c)

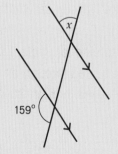

Angles of Polygons

Polygon Facts

You should know the following:
- A **polygon** is a shape made from straight sides, e.g. a **triangle**, a **quadrilateral**, a **pentagon**, and so on.
- **Interior angles** are the angles inside a polygon.
- **Exterior angles** are formed by extending one side of a polygon as shown in the diagram below.
- A **vertex** is a point where two sides meet, i.e. a corner.

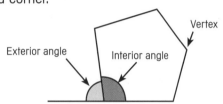

Vertex

Exterior angle

Interior angle

At any vertex:

| Interior angle + exterior angle = 180° |

Polygons can be divided into triangles. This hexagon has been divided into four triangles. So the sum of its interior angles is:

4 × 180° = 720°

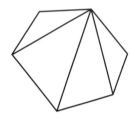

| Sum of interior angles of any polygon | = (number of sides – 2) × 180° |

Name	Triangle	Quadrilateral	Pentagon	Hexagon	Octagon	Decagon
Number of Sides	3	4	5	6	8	10
Sum of Interior Angles	180°	360°	540°	720°	1080°	1440°

Regular Polygons

A **regular polygon** has:
- all sides of equal length
- all interior angles of equal size
- all exterior angles of equal size
- line symmetry, e.g. a regular hexagon has six sides and six lines of symmetry
- rotational symmetry, e.g. a regular hexagon has rotational symmetry of order 6.

Imagine you are walking around the edge of a regular hexagon. Each time you turn at a vertex, you turn through the exterior angle. To return to the start, you have turned through all six exterior angles and you have turned through 360°.

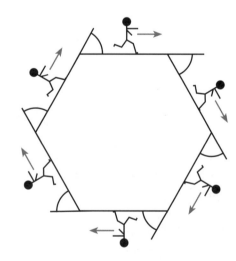

So:

| Number of sides × exterior angle = 360° |
| or |
| Exterior angle = $\dfrac{360°}{\text{number of sides}}$ |

Key Words   Polygon • Interior angle • Exterior angle • Vertex • Regular polygon

Example 1

Example 1

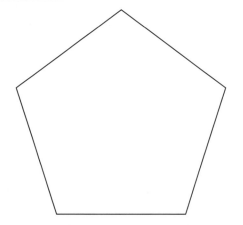

a) Work out the size of each exterior angle of a regular pentagon.

Solution

A regular pentagon has five sides.

Exterior angle of a regular pentagon is:

$\frac{360°}{5} = 72°$

b) Work out the size of each interior angle of a regular pentagon.

Solution

Interior angle + exterior angle = 180°

Interior angle of a regular pentagon is:
180° − 72° = 108°

Quick Test

1 Work out the size of the interior and exterior angles of these regular shapes:

a) Octagon   **b)** Decagon

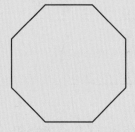   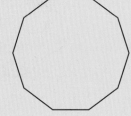

Example 2

The diagram shows a regular hexagon *ABCDEF*.
Work out the size of the angle marked x.

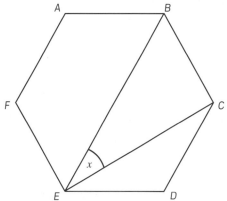

Solution

Problem Solving
Break this type of question into several steps. First find the exterior angle and use this to find the interior angle. Then use properties of isosceles triangles.

Exterior angle of a regular hexagon is:

$\frac{360°}{6} = 60°$

Interior angle + exterior angle = 180°

Interior angle of a regular hexagon is:
180° − 60° = 120°

So angle *FED* = 120°

EB bisects angle *FED*.

So angle *FEB* is $\frac{120°}{2} = 60°$

Triangle *EDC* is isosceles.

So angle *DEC* is $\frac{(180° - 120°)}{2} = 30°$

So x is 120° − 60° − 30° = 30°

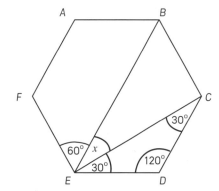

Perimeter and Area

Perimeter

The **perimeter** of a shape is the total distance around the outside edge.

A **compound shape** is a shape made up from other shapes such as squares, rectangles and triangles.

A common mistake when working out the perimeter of a compound shape is to include inside edges. Don't count any inside edges but remember to count all the outside edges.

Example

Two shapes, A and B, are shown on a centimetre square grid. Which has the greater perimeter?

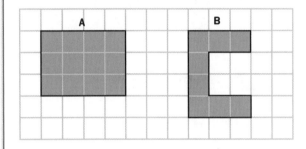

Solution

> **Problem Solving**
>
> It may help to number along the edges of the diagrams. It's not enough to just work out the perimeters. You have to state which is greater.

Perimeter of shape A is:

4 + 3 + 4 + 3 = 14 cm

Perimeter of shape B is:

3 + 1 + 2 + 2 + 2 + 1 + 3 + 4 = 18 cm

So shape B has the greater perimeter.

Area

To work out the **area** of a shape drawn on a centimetre square grid, just count the squares.

To estimate the area of an **irregular shape**:

1. count the whole squares
2. pair up areas that are more than half a square (✔) with areas that are less than half a square (✘)
3. estimate how many whole squares there are altogether.

Example

Estimate the area of the shape drawn on a centimetre grid.

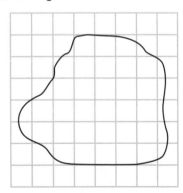

Solution

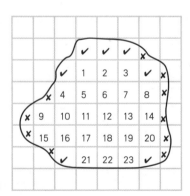

There are 23 whole squares and 7 or 8 pairs to match up, so the area is about 30 cm².

Surface Area and Nets

The **surface area** of a solid:

- is the total area of all the surfaces added together
- is equal to the area of the **net** of the shape.

Cube	Cuboid	Triangular Prism
The surface area of a cube is the total area of the six squares.	The surface area of a cuboid is the total area of the six faces.	The surface area of a triangular prism is the total area of the two triangles and the three rectangles.

Tessellations

A **tessellation** is a regular pattern of 2-D shapes that fit together:

- without overlaps
- without gaps.

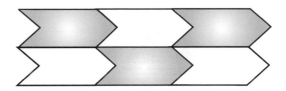

Quick Test

1 Work out **i)** the perimeter and **ii)** the area of these shapes on the centimetre square grid.

a) **b)**

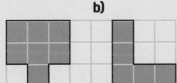

2 Estimate the area of the shape on the centimetre square grid.

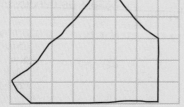

3 Sketch nets of the following:
  a) Cube
  b) Cuboid
  c) Square-based pyramid

4 Work out the total surface area of these shapes:

a)

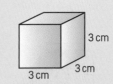

3 cm
3 cm 3 cm

b)

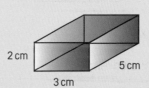

2 cm
5 cm
3 cm

c)

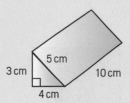

5 cm
3 cm 10 cm
4 cm

Areas of Triangles and Quadrilaterals

Area Calculations

Area of a Triangle

If you know the length of the base and the **perpendicular** height, you can use the following formula to work out the area of a triangle:

Area of triangle = $\frac{1}{2}$ × base × perpendicular height

$$A = \frac{1}{2}bh$$

or

Area of triangle = $\dfrac{\text{base × perpendicular height}}{2}$

$$A = \frac{bh}{2}$$

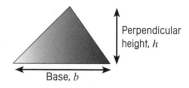

Perpendicular height, h

Base, b

Area of a Trapezium

Area of trapezium = $\frac{1}{2}(a + b)h$

N.B. This formula is given on the examination paper.

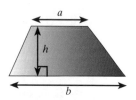

a

h

b

Area of a Parallelogram

$\dfrac{\text{Area of}}{\text{parallelogram}}$ = base × perpendicular height

$$A = bh$$

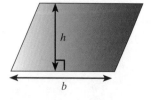

h

b

Example 1

Work out the area of these shapes.

a)

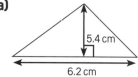

5.4 cm

6.2 cm

Solution

Area of triangle = $\dfrac{\text{base × perpendicular height}}{2}$

$= \dfrac{6.2 × 5.4}{2}$

$= 16.74 \text{ cm}^2$

b)

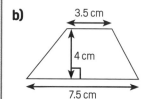

3.5 cm

4 cm

7.5 cm

Solution

Area of trapezium $= \frac{1}{2}(a + b)h$

$= \frac{1}{2}(3.5 + 7.5)4$

$= 22 \text{ cm}^2$

c)

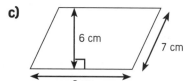

6 cm

7 cm

8 cm

Solution

Area of parallelogram $=$ base × perpendicular height

$= 8 × 6$

$= 48 \text{ cm}^2$

Don't mix up the perpendicular height with the sloping height

---

Example 2

The total area of this shape is 37.31 cm².

Work out the perpendicular height of the triangle.

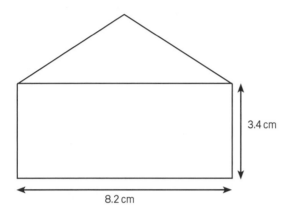

3.4 cm

8.2 cm

Solution

Problem Solving
You know the formula for the area of a triangle is $A = \frac{1}{2}bh$. You have all the information you need to find A and b, so then you can rearrange the formula to calculate h.

Area of rectangle is 8.2 × 3.4 = 27.88 cm²

Area of triangle is 37.31 − 27.88 = 9.43 cm²

Don't round values until the last step of the calculation otherwise your answer may be incorrect

$$\frac{\text{base} \times \text{perpendicular height}}{2} = 9.43$$

$$\frac{8.2 \times \text{perpendicular height}}{2} = 9.43$$

$$\text{Perpendicular height of triangle} = \frac{9.43 \times 2}{8.2}$$

$$= 2.3 \text{ cm}$$

Example 3

The area of the rectangle is three times the area of the triangle.

The total area of both shapes is 18 cm².

Work out the area of the triangle.

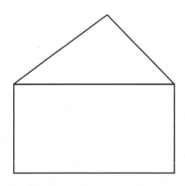

Solution

Problem Solving
Writing out the information you have been given in a mathematical way is a good starting point.

Let the area of the triangle be A cm².

So the area of the rectangle = $3A$ cm²

$$A + 3A = 18 \quad \leftarrow \text{Set up an equation}$$

$$4A = 18$$

$$A = 4.5 \quad \leftarrow \text{Divide both sides by 4}$$

So the area of the triangle is 4.5 cm²

Quick Test

1 Work out the areas of these shapes. Give your answers to 2 decimal places.

a)

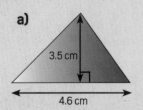

3.5 cm

4.6 cm

b)

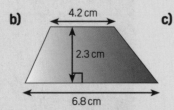

4.2 cm

2.3 cm

6.8 cm

c)

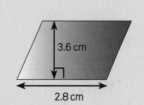

3.6 cm

2.8 cm

Circumference and Area of Circles

Circle Facts

You need to know the following:

- The **circumference** of a circle is the distance around the edge of the circle.
- The **radius** of a circle is a straight line from the centre to the circumference.
- The **diameter** is a straight line through the centre joining opposite points on the circumference.

- A **chord** is a straight line joining any two points on the circumference.
- A **tangent** is a straight line that touches the circumference of a circle.
- An **arc** is a part of the circumference of a circle.
- A **sector** is the area enclosed by two radii and an arc.
- A **segment** is the area between a chord and its arc.

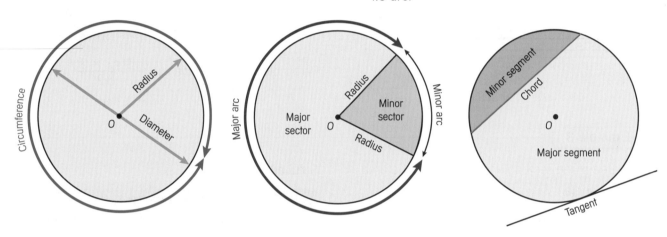

Calculations with Circles

Circumference of a Circle

Circumference is the word used to mean the **perimeter** of a circle.

The circumference of a circle is given by:

> **Circumference = π × diameter**
>
> $C = \pi d$
>
> or
>
> **Circumference = 2 × π × radius**
>
> $C = 2\pi r$

Area of a Circle

The area of a circle is given by:

> **Area = π × radius²**
>
> $A = \pi r^2$

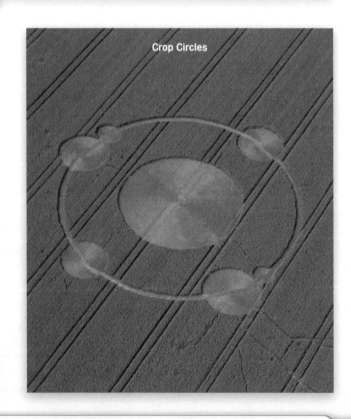

Crop Circles

Example 1

a) Work out the circumference of this circle. Give your answer to 2 decimal places.

5.4 cm

O

Solution

$C = 2\pi r$

$= 2 \times \pi \times 5.4$

$= 33.929...$

$= 33.93$ cm

> Remember to write down more than 2 decimal places before rounding

> You could get the same answer by working out the diameter ($2 \times 5.4 = 10.8$ cm), then using the formula $C = \pi d$

b) Work out the area of the circle. Give your answer to 2 decimal places.

Solution

$A = \pi r^2 = \pi \times 5.4 \times 5.4$

$= 91.608...$

$= 91.61$ cm^2

Example 2

a) Work out the circumference of this circle. Give your answer in terms of π.

8 cm

O

Solution

$C = 2\pi r$

$= 2 \times \pi \times 8$

$= 16\pi$ cm

> Again, you could get the same answer by working out the diameter ($2 \times 8 = 16$ cm), then using the formula $C = \pi d$. If you're asked to give an answer in terms of π, then leave the π symbol in your answer

b) Work out the area of the circle. Give your answer in terms of π.

Solution

$A = \pi r^2 = \pi \times 8 \times 8$

$= 64\pi$ cm^2

Example 3

Work out the perimeter of this semicircle. Give your answer to 2 decimal places.

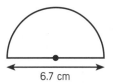

6.7 cm

Solution

Problem Solving
When asked to work out the perimeter, remember to calculate all the lengths of the shape you are given (in this case the length of the circular arc of the semicircle plus the diameter).

Length of circular arc $= \frac{1}{2}(\pi \times 6.7) = 10.524...$

Perimeter is length of circular arc + diameter =
$10.524... + 6.7$

$= 17.22$ cm

Quick Test

1. Work out **i)** the circumference and **ii)** the area of these circles. Give your answers to 1 decimal place.
   a) A circle of radius 4.7 cm
   b) A circle of diameter 6.1 cm
   c) A circle of radius 2.4 cm

2. Work out **i)** the circumference and **ii)** the area of these circles. Give your answers in terms of π.
   a) A circle of diameter 10 cm
   b) A circle of radius 6 cm

Plan and Elevation

Plan and Elevation

A **plan view** of a 3-D shape is what you see when you look at it from above.

The **front elevation** of a 3-D shape is what you see when you look at it from the front.

The **side elevation** of a 3-D shape is what you see when you look at it from the side.

Example 1

Here is a 3-D shape made of centimetre cubes drawn on isometric paper:

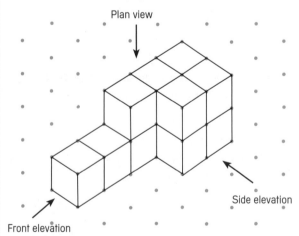

Draw **a)** the plan view, **b)** the front elevation and **c)** the side elevation on squared paper.

Solution

a)

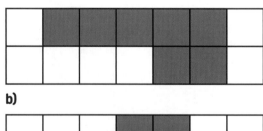

b)

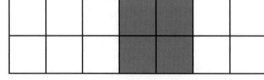

c)

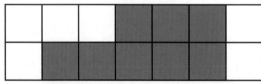

Example 2

Here are the three views of a 3-D shape:

Plan view

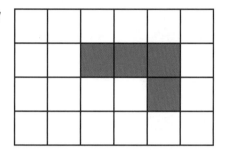

Front elevation

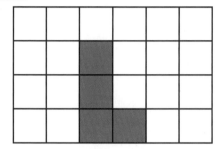

Side elevation

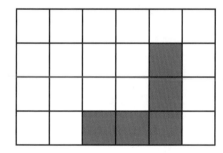

Draw the 3-D shape on isometric paper.

Solution

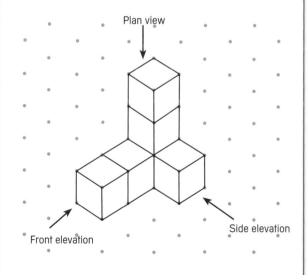

Quick Test

1. For each shape draw on squared paper:
   i) the plan view
   ii) the front elevation
   iii) the side elevation.

a)

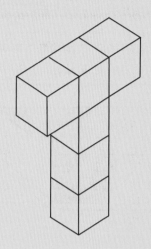

b)

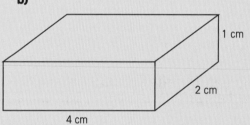

c)

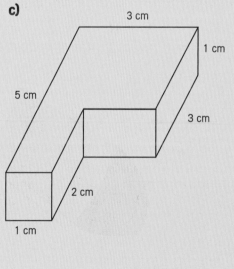

Volumes of Prisms

Volume Facts

You should know the following:

- **Volume** is the amount of space a 3-D shape fills.
- Common units for volume are cm^3 and m^3.

Volume of a Cuboid

> **Volume of a cuboid = length × width × height**
>
> $$V = lwh$$

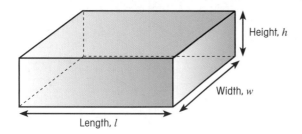

Length, l · Width, w · Height, h

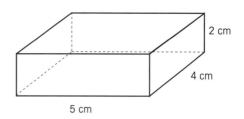

Example

Work out the volume of this cuboid.

2 cm
4 cm
5 cm

Solution

Volume of cuboid = length × width × height

Volume = 5 × 4 × 2

= 40 cm^3

Volume of a Prism

A **prism** is a 3-D shape that has **uniform cross-section**.

> **Volume of a prism = area of cross-section × length**
>
> $$V = Al$$
>
> *N.B. You're given this formula in the examination.*

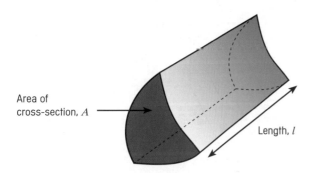

Area of cross-section, A · Length, l

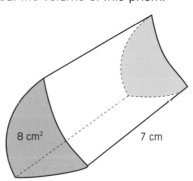

Example

Work out the volume of this prism.

8 cm^2
7 cm

Solution

Volume of prism = area of cross-section × length

Volume = 8 × 7

= 56 cm^3

Volumes of Cylinders and Triangular Prisms

Cylinders and **triangular prisms** are special types of prism.

The cross-section of a cylinder is a circle, so:
- the area of the circle (πr^2) is the area of the cross-section
- the volume of a cylinder = area of circle × height ($V = \pi r^2 h$)

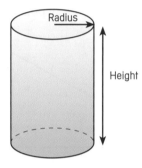
Radius
Height

The cross-section of a triangular prism is a triangle, so:
- the area of the triangle ($\frac{1}{2}$ × base × height) is the area of the cross-section
- the volume of a triangular prism = area of triangle × length

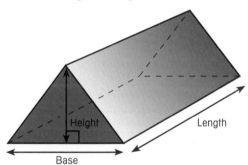
Height
Length
Base

Quick Test

1 Work out the volumes of these solids:
   a) A prism with cross-section 12 cm² and length 5 cm.
   b) A cylinder of height 4.2 cm and radius 6.1 cm.
   c) A triangular prism with base 4 cm, perpendicular height 3 cm and length 7 cm.

Example 1

Work out the volume of a cylinder of radius 4 cm and height 10 cm.

Solution

Volume of cylinder = $\pi \times 4^2 \times 10$ ← Area of circle × height

= 160π cm³ or 502.7 cm³

Example 2

Work out the volume of this triangular prism.

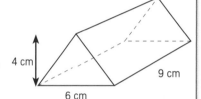
4 cm
9 cm
6 cm

Solution

Area of triangle = $\frac{1}{2} \times 6 \times 4$ ← $\frac{1}{2}$ × base × height

= 12 cm²

Volume of prism = 12 × 9 ← Area of cross-section × length

= 108 cm³

Example 3

You are given that 1 litre = 1000 cm³

A cylindrical water tank is $\frac{1}{4}$ full. How many more litres of water are needed to fill the tank?

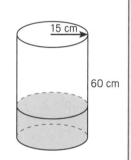
15 cm
60 cm

Solution

Problem Solving

Work out the volume of the whole shape, then work out the fraction you need. In this case you need $\frac{3}{4}$ of the total volume.

Volume of full tank = $\pi \times 15 \times 15 \times 60$

= 42 412 cm³

Volume of $\frac{3}{4}$ of tank is $\frac{42\,412}{4} \times 3 = 31\,809$ cm³

So approximately 31.8 litres are needed to fill the tank.

Pythagoras' Theorem

The Hypotenuse

The **hypotenuse** is:
- the **longest side** on a **right-angled triangle**
- opposite the right angle.

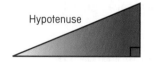 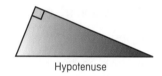

Pythagoras' Theorem

Pythagoras' theorem states that the square on the hypotenuse is equal to the sum of the squares on the other two sides. So $c^2 = a^2 + b^2$

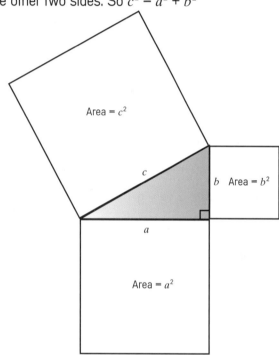

Example 1

Work out the length of the hypotenuse in this right-angled triangle.

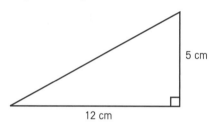

5 cm

12 cm

Solution

Pythagoras' theorem states that $c^2 = a^2 + b^2$

So $c^2 = 12^2 + 5^2$

$c^2 = 144 + 25$

$c^2 = 169$

So $c = \sqrt{169}$

$c = 13$ cm

Example 2

Work out the perimeter of this triangle. Give your answer to 1 decimal place.

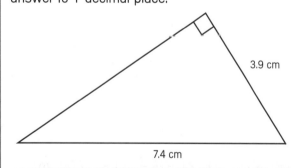

3.9 cm

7.4 cm

Problem Solving

You need to use Pythagoras' theorem in a right-angled triangle to work out the missing side.

Solution

$x^2 + 3.9^2 = 7.4^2$

$x^2 = 7.4^2 - 3.9^2$

$x^2 = 54.76 - 15.21$

$x^2 = 39.55$

So $x = \sqrt{39.55}$

$x = 6.2888\ldots$

So perimeter is $7.4 + 3.9 + 6.2888 = 17.588\ldots$ cm

$= 17.6$ cm

Hypotenuse • Pythagoras' theorem

Pythagorean Triples

A **Pythagorean triple** is where the values of a, b and c are all whole numbers. Some examples of these right-angled triangles are:

- 3, 4, 5
- 6, 8, 10
- 5, 12, 13
- 7, 24, 25
- 8, 15, 17

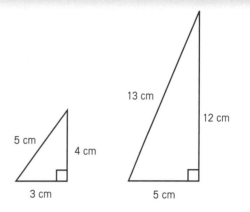

Example

Work out the area of this isosceles triangle.

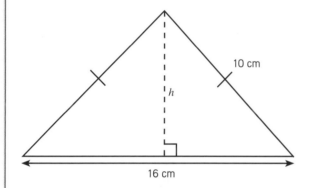

Problem Solving

An isosceles triangle can be broken up into two right-angled triangles, so you can use Pythagoras' theorem to work out the height. You then have all the information you need to work out the area.

Solution

$$10^2 = h^2 + 8^2$$

$$100 = h^2 + 64$$

$$100 - 64 = h^2$$

$$36 = h^2$$

So $h = 6$ cm

You may have spotted this is a Pythagorean triple. If so, you can just state the height is 6 cm because it's a 6, 8, 10 Pythagorean triple

Area $= \frac{1}{2} \times 16 \times 6$

$\frac{1}{2} \times$ base $\times$ height

Area $= 48$ cm^2

Quick Test

1 Work out the length of the missing sides in these right-angled triangles.

a)

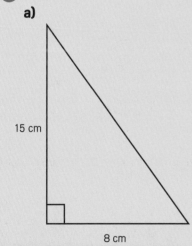

b)

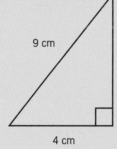

c)

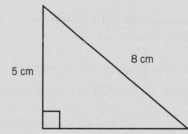

Transformations

Types of Transformation

A **transformation** changes the appearance of a shape. It may change the shape's **position**, **size** or **orientation**.

You'll need to draw or describe **reflections**, **rotations**, **translations** and **enlargements** of 2-D shapes. The original shape is called the **object**. The transformed shape is called the **image**.

Reflections

A **reflection** transforms a shape so that it's a **mirror image** of the original shape. The object and the image have line symmetry.

To describe a reflection you have to state the position of the mirror line, e.g. a reflection in the x-axis or a reflection in the line $x = 2$

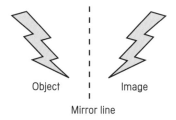

Each point on the object is the same distance from the mirror line as its corresponding point on the image

Rotations

A **rotation** transforms a shape so that the original shape is **turned about** a fixed point. The fixed point is called the **centre of rotation**.

To describe a rotation you have to state:
* the angle turned with the direction of turn (clockwise or anticlockwise)
* the centre of rotation.

For example, a rotation 90° clockwise about (0, 0) or a rotation 180° about (3, 2).

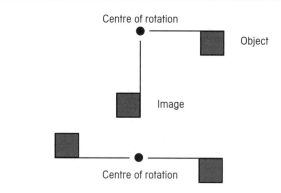

Each point on the object is the same distance from the centre of rotation as its corresponding point on the image

Translations

A **translation** transforms a shape so that the original shape **moves** without reflecting or rotating.

To describe a translation you have to state:
* the distance moved horizontally
* the distance moved vertically.

This can be written in words, e.g. 3 units to the right and 2 units down, or 4 units to the left and 5 units up.

Translations can also be written as **vectors**, e.g. $\begin{pmatrix} 3 \\ -2 \end{pmatrix}$ and $\begin{pmatrix} -4 \\ 5 \end{pmatrix}$:
* The top number is the horizontal movement (right is positive and left is negative).
* The bottom number is the vertical movement (up is positive and down is negative).

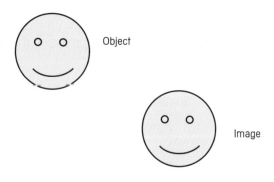

Every point in the shape moves in the same direction and through the same distance

Enlargements

An **enlargement** transforms a shape so that the original shape **increases** or **decreases** in size. The **scale factor** of an enlargement shows how the lengths of a shape increase or decrease, e.g. for a scale factor 2, the lengths double.

To describe an enlargement you have to state:
- the centre of enlargement
- the scale factor of the enlargement.

For example, an enlargement, centre (0, 0), scale factor 2.

Example 1

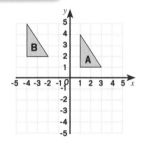

a) Describe the single transformation that takes triangle A to triangle B.

Solution
Translation 5 units to the left and 1 unit up or translation $\binom{-5}{1}$

b) Reflect triangle A in the line $y = -x$. Label it C.

Solution

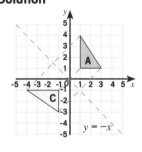

Example 2

Enlarge triangle A with scale factor 2 and centre of enlargement (0, 1). Label it B.

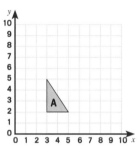

Solution

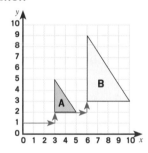

Example 3

Triangle A is translated $\binom{-5}{0}$ to form triangle B. Triangle B is then rotated 180° about the origin to form triangle C. Describe the single transformation that takes triangle A to triangle C.

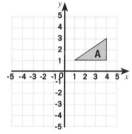

Solution

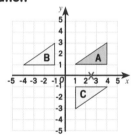

Triangle A to triangle C is a rotation of 180° about (2.5, 0).

Quick Test

 1 Copy this diagram.

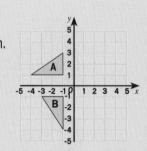

a) Translate triangle A by the vector $\binom{6}{-1}$. Label it C.

b) Reflect triangle A in the line $y = x$. Label it D.

c) Describe the single transformation that takes triangle A to triangle B.

d) Describe the single transformation that takes triangle B to triangle D.

Basic Measures

Measuring Lines and Reading Scales

You need to be able to read scales in lots of different situations, such as when using:

- a ruler
- a thermometer
- kitchen scales
- a speedometer.

Example 1

Measure these lines:

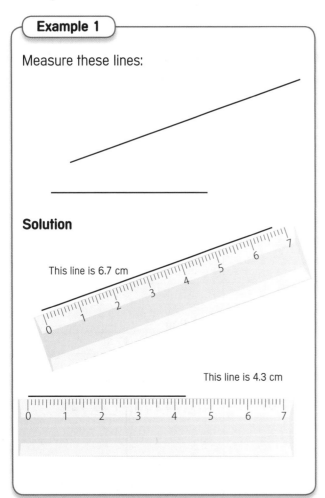

Solution

This line is 6.7 cm

This line is 4.3 cm

Example 2

Write down the values shown by each scale.

a)

Solution

The scale goes up by 1°C each time so the temperature is −7°C.

b)

Solution

The scale goes up by 20 grams each time so the reading is 140 grams.

c)

Solution

The scale goes up by 2 mph each time and it's pointing between 24 mph and 26 mph, so the speed is 25 mph.

Measuring Angles

When you measure angles using a protractor:

- always measure from 0
- check whether your angle is **acute** (less than 90°) or **obtuse** (between 90° and 180°).

To measure a **reflex** angle:

1. measure the other angle
2. subtract this angle from 360°.

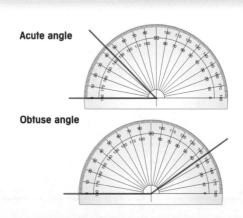

Acute angle

This angle measures 45°

Obtuse angle

This angle measures 145°

Example

Work out the size of the reflex angle.

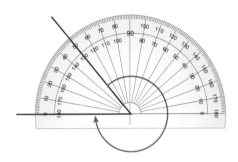

Solution

The acute angle is 50° so the reflex angle is:

360° − 50° = 310°

Timetables

Timetables often use the **24-hour clock**.

This timetable shows the times for five trains from Doncaster to King's Cross. Some trains don't stop at all the stations.

Doncaster	12.24	13.16	13.45	13.53	14.23
Retford	12.39	—	—	—	14.39
Grantham	13.07	—	14.16	—	15.06
Peterborough	13.27	14.07	—	14.52	15.27
King's Cross	14.26	15.02	15.28	15.45	16.24

Look at the timetable and check these facts:

- The 12.24 from Doncaster arrives at King's Cross at 14.26, or 2.26pm using the **12-hour clock**.
- The 13.16 from Doncaster doesn't stop at Retford or Grantham.
- The 13.45 from Doncaster takes 31 minutes to get to Grantham.
- The 13.53 from Doncaster arrives at Peterborough at eight minutes to 3.
- The 14.23 from Doncaster takes more than two hours to get to King's Cross.

Quick Test

1. Read this scale:

2. Measure these lines:
   a) ————————
   b) /

3. Measure these angles:
   a)

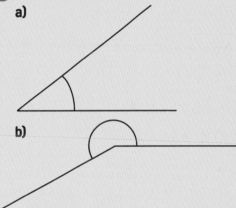

   b)

4. Use the Doncaster to King's Cross timetable opposite to answer the following questions.
   a) I want to arrive at King's Cross before 4pm. What is the latest of the five trains I can catch from Doncaster?
   b) How long does the 13.16 from Doncaster take to get to Peterborough?
   c) Which trains from Doncaster don't stop at Grantham?
   d) Abdul lives 25 minutes' walk from Doncaster station. He leaves home at 1pm. He catches the first train that he can. What time should he arrive at King's Cross?

Conversion and Estimation

Conversions

For the examination you need to learn these **conversions** from **metric** to **imperial** measurements:

- 1 kg ≈ 2.2 pounds
- 1 litre ≈ $1\frac{3}{4}$ pints
- 4.5 litres ≈ 1 gallon
- 8 km ≈ 5 miles
- 30 cm ≈ 1 foot

You should also know common metric conversions:

Length	1 m = 100 cm
	1 km = 1000 m
	1 m = 1000 mm
	1 cm = 10 mm
Mass	1 tonne = 1000 kg
	1 kg = 1000 g

Example 1

Convert 56 km to miles.

Solution

8 km ≈ 5 miles

So 1 km ≈ $\frac{5}{8}$ mile ← Divide by 8

56 km is $\frac{5}{8}$ × 56 = 35 miles ← Multiply by 56

Example 2

Use the graph to convert:

a) 16 gallons into litres

b) 40 litres into gallons

Solution

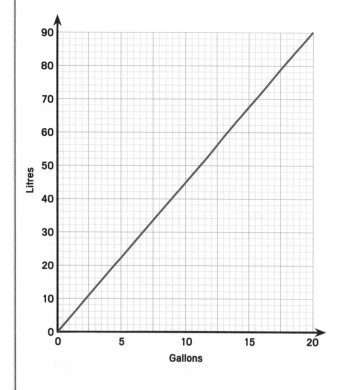

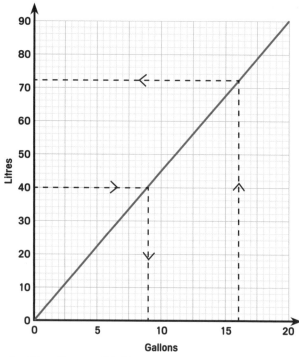

a) 16 gallons ≈ 72 litres

b) 40 litres ≈ 9 gallons

Estimating Measures

It's useful to be able to **estimate** the length, area, volume or weight of everyday objects.

You should know that:
- a long ruler is 30 cm
- a man is about 1.8 metres tall
- a bag of sugar weighs about 1 kg
- a can of petrol holds about 5 litres.

You can use these facts to make other estimates.

Example 1

Estimate the height of the bus.

Solution

The bus is three times the height of the man.

A man is about 1.8 metres tall.

So the height of the bus is about:
1.8 × 3 = 5.4 m

Example 2

Estimate the weight of one apple in grams.

Solution

Sugar weighs 1 kg or 1000 grams.

So one apple will be about

1000 ÷ 5 = 200 grams

On the scales, five apples are balanced with the bag of sugar

Quick Test

1. Convert:
   a) 5 kg into pounds
   b) 15 miles into kilometres
   c) 4 gallons into litres
2. Write down a suitable metric unit to measure each of the following.
   a) The distance between two towns
   b) The amount of fuel in a car tank
   c) The amount of butter in a dish

Constructions

Accurate Drawings

A **construction** is an accurate drawing using a combination of ruler, protractor and a pair of compasses. In your examination it's important that when you use a pair of compasses, the construction arcs are clearly shown and that all lengths and angles are accurate.

Example 1

a) Construct triangle ABC with AB = 3 cm, BC = 2.5 cm and AC = 2 cm

Solution

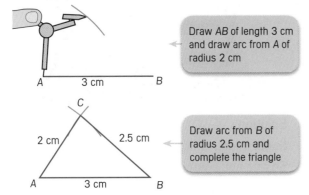

Draw AB of length 3 cm and draw arc from A of radius 2 cm

Draw arc from B of radius 2.5 cm and complete the triangle

b) Construct triangle ABC with AB = 3 cm, AC = 2 cm and angle BAC = 70°

Solution

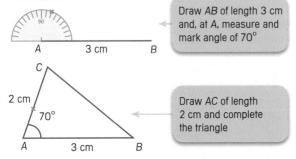

Draw AB of length 3 cm and, at A, measure and mark angle of 70°

Draw AC of length 2 cm and complete the triangle

c) Construct triangle ABC with AB = 2 cm, AC = 2 cm and angle ABC = 50°

Solution

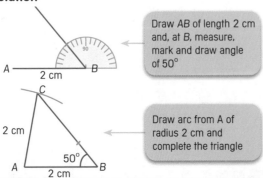

Draw AB of length 2 cm and, at B, measure, mark and draw angle of 50°

Draw arc from A of radius 2 cm and complete the triangle

Example 2

a) Use a ruler and a pair of compasses only to construct an angle of 60°.

Solution

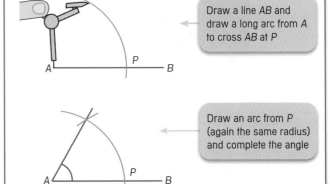

Draw a line AB and draw a long arc from A to cross AB at P

Draw an arc from P (again the same radius) and complete the angle

b) Use a ruler and a pair of compasses only to construct an angle of 90°.

Solution

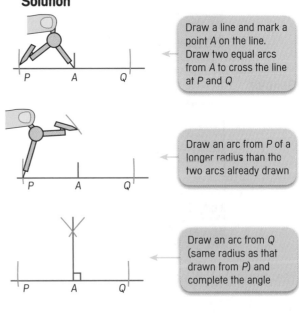

Draw a line and mark a point A on the line. Draw two equal arcs from A to cross the line at P and Q

Draw an arc from P of a longer radius than the two arcs already drawn

Draw an arc from Q (same radius as that drawn from P) and complete the angle

Example 3

a) Draw a line *AB*. Construct the **perpendicular bisector** of the line *AB*.

Solution

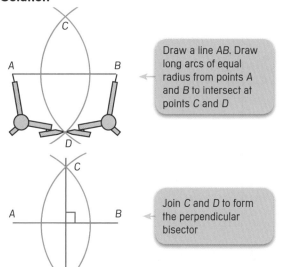

Draw a line *AB*. Draw long arcs of equal radius from points *A* and *B* to intersect at points *C* and *D*

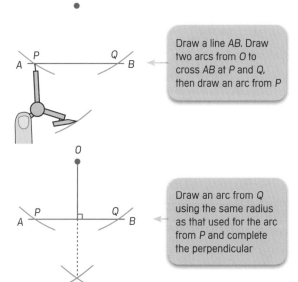

Join *C* and *D* to form the perpendicular bisector

b) Draw a line *AB*. Construct a perpendicular from a point *O* above the line.

Solution

Draw a line *AB*. Draw two arcs from *O* to cross *AB* at *P* and *Q*, then draw an arc from *P*

Draw an arc from *Q* using the same radius as that used for the arc from *P* and complete the perpendicular

c) Draw an angle. Construct the angle bisector.

Solution

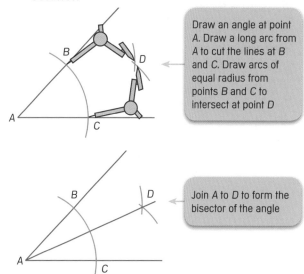

Draw an angle at point *A*. Draw a long arc from *A* to cut the lines at *B* and *C*. Draw arcs of equal radius from points *B* and *C* to intersect at point *D*

Join *A* to *D* to form the bisector of the angle

d) Construct an angle of 30°.

Solution

Problem Solving

Think about how you can combine basic constructions. In this case, construct an angle of 60° and then bisect it to create an angle half the size.

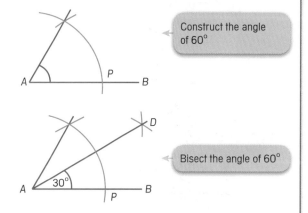

Construct the angle of 60°

Bisect the angle of 60°

Quick Test

1. Construct a triangle *ABC* with *AB* = 8 cm, *BC* = 6.5 cm and *AC* = 5.7 cm
2. Construct an angle of 45°.

Bearings and Loci

Bearings

A **bearing** gives the direction to one place from another.

To measure a **three-figure bearing**:
- start from North
- measure clockwise

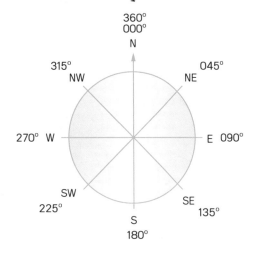

Three-figure bearings should always be given using three digits, e.g. a bearing of 45° is written 045°.

Example

The diagram shows a map drawn to scale showing two towns, A and B.

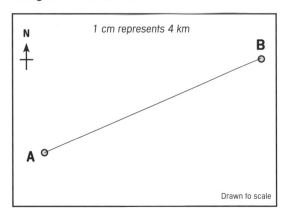

a) Work out the bearing and the actual distance from A to B.

Solution

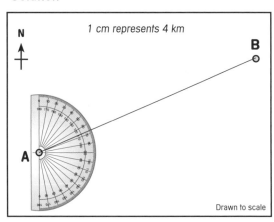

Bearing is 067°
AB on the map is 6.4 cm, so the actual distance is 6.4 × 4 = 25.6 km

b) Work out the bearing of A from B.

Solution
067° + 180° = 247°

If two bearings are in opposite directions, the difference between the bearings is 180°

Bearing • Three-figure bearing

Loci

A **locus** (plural: **loci**) is a path made by a set of points that follow a rule.

Here are some facts about loci:

The locus of points that are a fixed distance from a fixed point is a circle.

The locus of points that are a fixed distance from a fixed line is a pair of parallel lines with a semicircle at either end.

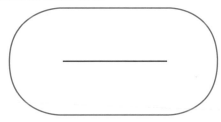

The locus of points that are a fixed distance from two fixed points is the perpendicular bisector of the line joining the points.

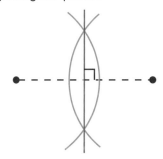

The locus of points that are a fixed distance from two fixed lines is the angle bisector of the two lines.

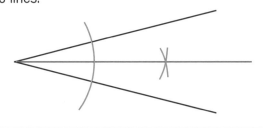

Example

A goat is tied to the corner of a building by a rope 4 metres long. Show the area that the goat can reach on the diagram.

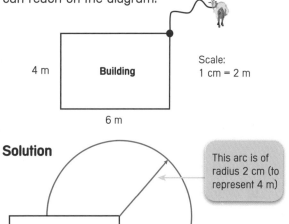

Solution

This arc is of radius 2 cm (to represent 4 m)

Quick Test

1. Sketch bearings of:
   a) 030°   **b)** 140°   **c)** 270°

2. A goat is tied to a post in each field by a rope 5 m long. Describe or draw the locus of the shape the goat can reach. The diagrams are drawn to a scale of 1 cm = 2 m

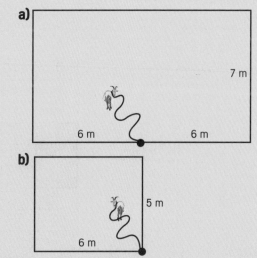

You may wish to answer these questions on a separate piece of paper so that you can show full working out, which you will be expected to do in the exam.

 1. Here is an L-shape on centimetre-squared grid paper:

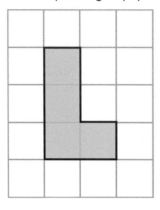

a) Write down the area. **(1)**

.... cm²

b) Work out the perimeter. **(2)**

.... cm

2. **a)** Reflect the shaded shape in the mirror line. **(1)**

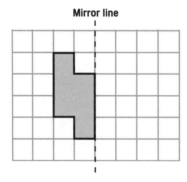

b) On the grid draw an enlargement, scale factor 2, of the shaded shape. **(2)**

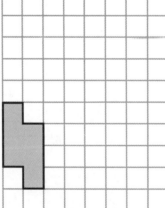

3. The diagram shows a parallelogram.

Write down the order of rotational symmetry. **(1)**

....

4. **a)** Work out the size of the angle marked x. **(2)**

.... °

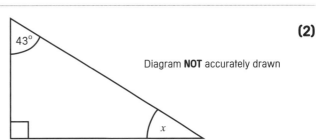

Diagram **NOT** accurately drawn

b) Work out the size of the angle marked y. **(3)**

.... °

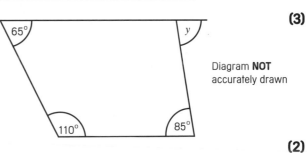

Diagram **NOT**
accurately drawn

5. Work out the area of the triangle. **(2)**

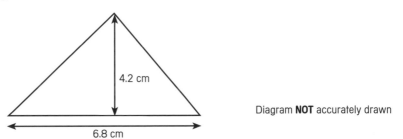

Diagram **NOT** accurately drawn

....

6. Work out the area of the trapezium. **(2)**

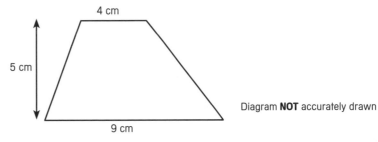

Diagram **NOT** accurately drawn

....

7.

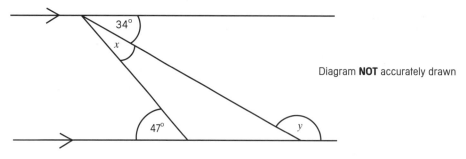

Diagram **NOT** accurately drawn

a) Work out the value of x. **(2)**

b) Work out the value of y. **(2)**

8. Work out the area of a circle of radius 4 cm. Give your answer in cm² to 1 decimal place. **(3)**

9. A ship sails 20 miles north from a port (P) to a lighthouse (L).

It then turns and sails 25 miles east to an oil rig (R). It then returns directly to the port.

a) Make a sketch of the route sailed by the ship. **(2)**

b) Work out the distance from the oil rig back to the port. Give your answer to a suitable degree of accuracy. **(3)**

10.

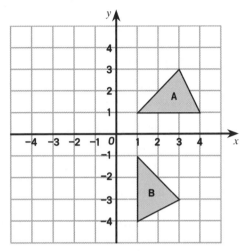

Describe fully the single transformation that maps triangle A to triangle B. **(3)**

---

11. Work out the perimeter of this semicircle. Give your answer in centimetres to 2 decimal places. **(3)**

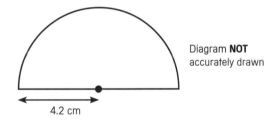

Diagram **NOT** accurately drawn

4.2 cm

---

12. The diagram shows a solid metal cylinder and an open cuboid.

The cylinder is melted down and the metal is poured into the cuboid.

Work out the height of the metal in the cuboid. **(5)**

Diagram **NOT** accurately drawn

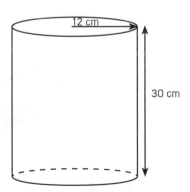

12 cm

30 cm

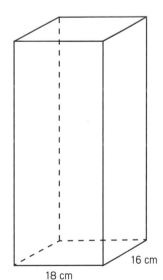

16 cm

18 cm

Handling Data Cycle and Questionnaires

The Handling Data Cycle

Statistics is about the collection, organisation and interpretation of data.

A **hypothesis** is an idea or assumption which is then tested to decide whether it's true or false. To test a hypothesis the **handling data cycle** is used.

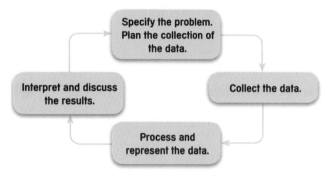

To use the handling data cycle:
- state a hypothesis, outlining the problem and planning the task
- plan the data collection and collect the data
- process the data using statistical calculations, e.g. mean and range (see page 78)
- interpret the data and make conclusions.

The final step includes reviewing the task, refining it and continuing the cycle if necessary.

Data Collection

You need to know these terms:
- **Primary data** is data that you collect.
- **Secondary data** is data that has already been collected by someone else.
- **Discrete data** can only have certain values in a given range, e.g. number of goals scored: 0, 1, 2, 3, and so on. It's not possible to have half a goal!
- **Continuous data** can have any value within a given range, e.g. height of a person: 1.83... metres.
- A **survey** is an organised way of collecting data.
- A **questionnaire** is one way of carrying out a survey.

- **Observations** in an **experiment** are another way of carrying out a survey.
- A **population** is all the group you're investigating.
- A **sample** is a part of the population you're investigating.

To collect the data:
1. decide whether to use the population or a sample
2. carry out a survey or an experiment
3. record the results in a suitable way, e.g. use a tally chart or a frequency table.

Processing and Representing the Data

To process and represent the data:
- a suitable average could be calculated (mode, median or mean)
- a suitable measure of spread could be calculated (range)
- suitable statistical charts, diagrams or graphs could be drawn.

Key Words   Hypothesis • Primary data • Secondary data • Discrete data • Continuous data

Handling Data Cycle and Questionnaires

Interpreting and Discussing Results

Results are interpreted and discussed in order to:
- make comparisons
- draw conclusions
- decide whether the hypothesis is true, not true or inconclusive
- decide whether to refine the hypothesis or continue with the cycle.

Example

A farmer wants to compare two types of lettuce, A and B, to decide which is better. Describe the handling data cycle that he could use.

Solution

Problem Solving
Think about what he would want to know and how he would collect the data. Then set out the information in a logical way.

State a hypothesis:

Lettuce A grows faster than lettuce B.

Plan the data collection and collect the data:

Plant a tray of each seed and store in the same conditions to avoid bias.

After two weeks measure the plants and record the results.

Process and represent the data:
- Work out the mean height of lettuces in each tray.

Interpret and discuss the results:
- Look at the results and compare the means.
- Decide whether there are any significant differences by referring to the context of the hypothesis.
- State how to improve the cycle, e.g. use a larger sample of seeds or measure after a different period of time.

Questionnaires

Any question written as part of a questionnaire for a survey should:
- be as simple as possible
- allow anyone asked to give an answer
- have responses that don't overlap and have no gaps
- not be a leading, personal or irrelevant question.

Quick Test

1. Ali thinks that boys are better than girls at spelling in his class. How could he use the handling data cycle to test his hypothesis?

2. Criticise this question:
   Do you agree that fast food is bad for you?
   ❏ Yes ❏ No

Example

Here is a question from a questionnaire about eating out. Give two criticisms of the response section.

How many times do you eat out each week?
❏ 1–3   ❏ 3–6   ❏ More than 7

Solution

3 could be in the first or second box. — Response options overlap

It's not possible to answer 0 or 7 times. — Gaps in the response options

Averages and Range

Mode, Median, Mean and Range

An **average** is a measure used to represent a set of data. The most commonly used averages are:

- the **mode** – the most common value (**MO**de is **MO**st)
- the **median** – the middle value of the ordered data or halfway between the middle two values for an even number of values (**MeD**ian is **MiD**dle)

- **mean** – given by the formula:

$$\text{Mean} = \frac{\text{sum of the values}}{\text{number of values}}$$

(Me**AN** is add up **AN**d divide)

The **range** measures the spread of the data.

$$\boxed{\text{Range} = \text{biggest value} - \text{smallest value}}$$

Example 1

Here is the number of goals scored in nine matches:

    4   0   2   3   5   2   2   6   3

Work out the mode, median, mean and range.

Solution

Mode is the most common = 2 goals

Writing the numbers in order gives:

0   2   2   2   3   3   4   5   6

Median is the middle value = 3 goals

Mean is $\frac{0+2+2+2+3+3+4+5+6}{9} = \frac{27}{9} = 3$ goals

Range is $6 - 0 = 6$ goals

Example 2

Find five numbers with a range of 6 and a mean of 4.

Solution

> **Problem Solving**
> Work out the sum of the numbers using the mean. Here the sum of the numbers is five times the mean as there are five numbers.

Sum of the numbers is $4 \times 5 = 20$

Written in order the first and last numbers have a difference of 6.

2 … … … 8

> Trying 2 and 8 means the other three numbers add up to 10

So 2 3 3 4 8 works.

> There are lots of other answers. Can you find a different answer?

Mode, Median, Mean and Range from a Frequency Table

The mode, median, mean and range can be worked out from a **frequency** table.

Example

Work out the mode, median, mean and range of the number of children per family.

Number of Children (x)	Frequency (f)	Frequency × Number of Children (fx)
0	4	0
1	6	6
2	9	18
3	1	3
	Total = 20	Total = 27

Solution

Mode (most common) is 2 children per family.

The median is the middle of the 20 values, which is halfway between the 10th and 11th values.

> Listing in order:
> 0, 0, 0, 0, 1, 1, 1, 1, 1, (1, 2), 2, 2, 2, 2, 2, 2, 2, 3

10th value = 1, 11th value = 2, so median = 1.5 children per family

> Sum of values ÷ number of values

Mean is $\frac{27}{20} = 1.35$ children per family

Range is $3 - 0 = 3$ children per family

Grouped Data

The **modal class** is the class with the biggest frequency. The class containing the median is the class that contains the middle value. To estimate the mean, mid-values are used to represent each class.

Example

Recorded Temp. T (°C)	Frequency (f)	Mid-Temp. Values (x)	Frequency × Mid-Temp. Values (fx)
$10 \leqslant T < 15$	2	12.5	2 × 12.5 = 25
$15 \leqslant T < 20$	4	17.5	4 × 17.5 = 70
$20 \leqslant T < 25$	5	22.5	5 × 22.5 = 112.5
$25 \leqslant T < 30$	8	27.5	8 × 27.5 = 220
$30 \leqslant T < 35$	5	32.5	5 × 32.5 = 162.5
	Total = 24		**Total = 590**

These are class intervals

These are halfway values for the class intervals

a) Work out the modal class, the class that contains the median and an estimate of the mean for the recorded temperatures.

Solution

The modal class is $25°C \leqslant T < 30°C$

There are 24 temperatures altogether so the middle is halfway between the 12th and 13th temperatures.

The class containing these is $25°C \leqslant T < 30°C$

The individual temperatures aren't known so the mid-value of each group is used as an estimate.

Estimate of mean = $\dfrac{\text{total of recorded temperatures}}{\text{total frequency}}$

Estimate of mean is $\dfrac{590}{24}$ = 24.58°C

b) Explain why it's not possible to work out the range.

Solution

> **Problem Solving**
>
> Think about what you need to know to work out the range and what information is missing. Write your explanation clearly.

The lowest and highest temperatures aren't known, only that the lowest temperature is in the class $10°C \leqslant T < 15°C$ and the highest temperature is in the class $30°C \leqslant T < 35°C$.

Quick Test

1. Work out the mode, median, mean and range for this data.

   5 1 9 9 9 2 3 2

2. Work out the modal class, the class that contains the median and an estimate of the mean for this data.

x	f
$0 < x \leqslant 2$	10
$2 < x \leqslant 4$	21
$4 < x \leqslant 6$	13
$6 < x \leqslant 8$	7

Key Words   Modal class

Collecting and Sorting Data

Tally Charts and Frequency Tables

A **data collection sheet** is usually used to collect data:

- **Tallies** are usually grouped in fives, e.g. 卌 ‖ represents 5 + 2 = 7
- **Frequency** is the total for each group of tallies.

Here is a data collection sheet for how students get to school.

	Tally	Frequency
Walk	卌 ‖	7
Car	卌 ‖	6
Bus	‖‖	3
Cycle	卌 卌 卌	15

Stem and Leaf Diagrams

A **stem and leaf diagram** is used to sort discrete data into **ordered** groups.

Numbers in the **stem** (often the 'tens' digits) and numbers in the **leaves** (often the 'units' digits) are aligned to show the shape of the distribution.

Example

A student records the number of text messages she sends each day for 15 days.

21	32	31	10	18	19	25	37

30	34	22	25	34	32	25

a) Show the results in a stem and leaf diagram.

Solution A

10, 18, 19, 21, 22, 25, 25, ← Sort the numbers into order
25, 30, 31, 32, 32, 34, 34, 37

Stem   Leaves

```
1 | 0  8  9
2 | 1  2  5  5  (5)
3 | 0  1  2  2  4  4  7
```
Put the data into a stem and leaf diagram

1 | 0 represents 10 text messages ← Add a key

Solution B

```
1 | 0  8  9
2 | 1  5  2  5  5
3 | 2  1  7  0  4  4  2
```
Put the data into an unordered stem and leaf diagram

```
1 | 0  8  9
2 | 1  2  5  5  (5)
3 | 0  1  2  2  4  4  7
```
Reorder the values

1 | 0 represents 10 text messages ← Add a key

b) Work out the median.

Solution

The median of the 15 values is the 8th number (circled) when the numbers are ordered, so median = 25

Two-way Tables

A **two-way table** is a table that links two sets of information.

The table shows there are 83 boys and 62 girls in year 10 and 75 boys and 94 girls in year 11.

	Year 10	Year 11
Boys	83	75
Girls	62	94

Example

Complete the two-way table using this information about people visiting a theatre:

- Altogether there are 120 adults.
- There are twice as many male adults as female adults.
- Altogether there are 75 females.
- There are 65 male children.

	Male	Female	Total
Adults			
Children			
Total			

Solution

Problem Solving

First fill in the numbers you're given (in this case 120, 65 and 75). Now calculate the missing ones. You're given the total number of adults and the proportion of male adults to female adults, so you can use ratio to find these.

	Male	Female	Total
Adults	80	40	120
Children	65	35	100
Total	145	75	220

120 divided in the ratio
2 : 1 = 80 : 40

Quick Test

1. a) Show these lengths in an ordered stem and leaf diagram. Remember to complete a key.

   12 cm   14 cm   28 cm   25 cm
   22 cm   11 cm   12 cm   15 cm
   18 cm   25 cm   12 cm

   b) Work out the mode, median and range.

2. The two-way table shows the number of left-handed and right-handed boys and girls in a class.

   a) How many boys are in the class?

   b) A child is chosen at random.
   What is the probability that it's a left-handed girl?

	Left-handed	Right-handed
Boys	5	8
Girls	6	10

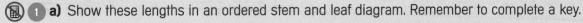

Representing Data

Graphs and Charts

Pictograms

A **pictogram** can be used to represent discrete data. A **key** is needed for each symbol.

Pictogram of Hours of Sunshine

Manchester	◯ ◯ ◖
Luxor	◯ ◯ ◯ ◯ ◯ ◯
Melbourne	◯ ◖

Key: ◯ = 2 hours of sunshine

Vertical Line Graphs and Bar Charts

A **vertical line graph** or a **bar chart** can be used to represent discrete data. The height of each line shows the frequency.

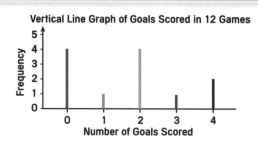

Line Graphs

A **line graph** can be used for discrete or continuous data. If the values between the plots have no meaning, the points should be joined with a dashed line as shown.

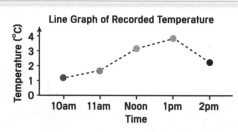

Multiple and Composite Bar Charts

A **multiple bar chart** and a **composite bar chart** show two or more groups of data:

- A multiple bar chart shows two or more groups of data side by side.
- A composite bar chart combines two or more groups of data into a single bar.

A key is needed for each group of data.

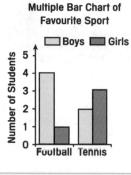

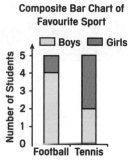

Histograms and Frequency Polygons

A **histogram** or a **frequency polygon** can be used to show continuous data.

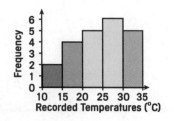

Histogram of Recorded Temperatures

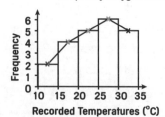

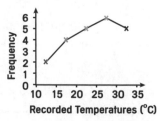

Frequency Polygon of Recorded Temperatures

Key Words Pictogram • Key • Vertical line graph • Bar chart • Line graph • Multiple bar chart • Composite bar chart

Representing Data

Pie Charts

A **pie chart** can be used to show how parts of a whole are made up. Each part is represented by a sector of a circle. The angle of each sector is proportional to the frequency it represents.

This table of data has been used to construct a pie chart.

Favourite Sport	Number of Students	Calculation	Angle
Football	7	$\frac{7}{18} \times 360°$	140°
Tennis	3	$\frac{3}{18} \times 360°$	60°
Hockey	8	$\frac{8}{18} \times 360°$	160°
	Total = 18		**Total = 360°**

Favourite Sport

Always check that the angles add up to 360°

Example

The frequency polygons show the lengths of time some students spend on a piece of work. Compare the times for boys and girls.

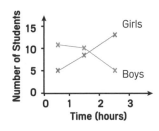

Mid-intervals × frequencies

Solution

More girls spent longer on the task.

Problem Solving
Write down any true facts but ensure you compare the same facts for boys and girls.

The total time for girls was approximately
$(5 \times 0.5 + 8 \times 1.5 + 13 \times 2.5)$ hours = 47 hours

The total time for boys was approximately
$(11 \times 0.5 + 10 \times 1.5 + 5 \times 2.5)$ hours = 33 hours

Scatter Diagrams

A **scatter diagram** (**scatter graph**) helps to compare two sets of data by plotting points to represent each pair of variables. **Correlation** describes any trend shown.

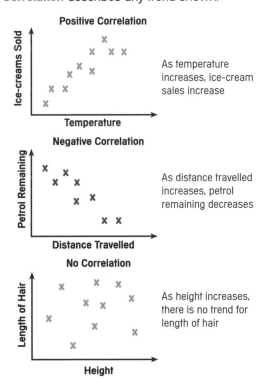

As temperature increases, ice-cream sales increase

As distance travelled increases, petrol remaining decreases

As height increases, there is no trend for length of hair

A **line of best fit**:
- is a straight line through the points
- can be used to estimate unknown values within the range of the points plotted
- is to show the trend – it doesn't have to pass exactly through any of the points.

The correlation is:
- **strong** if the points are very **close** to the line
- **weak** if the points are more widely **spread**.

Quick Test

1. The pictogram shows the number of boys attending revision classes.

Monday	⊞⊞⊞
Tuesday	⊞⊞⊞⊡
Wednesday	⊞⊞

⊞ represents 4 boys

a) How many boys attended on Monday?
b) How many more boys attended on Tuesday than on Wednesday?

Key Words   Histogram • Frequency polygon • Pie chart • Scatter diagram • Correlation • Line of best fit

83

Probability

Probability

Probability is the chance that something will happen.

Probabilities:
- lie on a scale from 0 to 1
- are fractions, decimals or percentages.

Words are often used to describe the **chance** of something happening. These words can be represented on a **probability scale**.

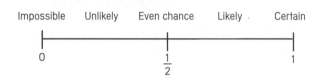

> **Example**
>
> Use probability words to describe these events.
>
> **a)** Someone in a class being right-handed.
>
> **Solution**
> Most people are right-handed so this is **likely**.
>
> **b)** It will rain in England this year.
>
> **Solution**
> It rains every year in England so this is **certain**.

Events and Outcomes

You need to know the following:
- An **event** is anything that you want to use to measure the probability of something happening, e.g. tossing a coin.
- An **outcome** is the result of an event, e.g. getting a head.

- P(A) means the probability of outcome A happening.
- **Equally likely outcomes** each have the same probability of happening, e.g. getting a head or a tail on a fair coin.

Probability of an Outcome

$$P(\text{outcome}) = \frac{\text{number of ways the outcome can happen}}{\text{total number of possible outcomes}}$$

> **Example**
>
> There are 8 boys and 7 girls in a team. The captain is chosen at random.
>
> Write down the probability the captain is a girl.
>
> **Solution**
> There are 7 girls out of 15 in the team, so
> $P(\text{girl}) = \frac{7}{15}$

Mutually Exclusive Events

Mutually exclusive events are events that have no outcomes in common, e.g. choosing an odd or an even number from a list.

If the probability of an outcome is p, the probability of the outcome not happening is $1 - p$.

Example

In a drawer there are only blue and black socks.

The probability of picking a black sock at random is $\frac{3}{5}$.

a) What is the probability of picking a blue sock?

Solution

P(blue) is $1 - \text{P(black)} = 1 - \frac{3}{5} = \frac{2}{5}$

b) There are 4 more black socks than blue socks. How many socks are in the drawer altogether?

Solution

> **Problem Solving**
>
> Start by working out what fraction 4 socks is of all the socks in the drawer. You can then use this fraction to work out the total number of socks.

The probability of picking a black sock is $\frac{1}{5}$ greater than picking a blue sock.

So the extra 4 socks must represent $\frac{3}{5} - \frac{2}{5} = \frac{1}{5}$ of the total socks in the drawer.

So there are 4 × 5

= 20 socks in the drawer ← 12 black and 8 blue

Quick Test

1. Match these probability words to their probabilities:

   Impossible $\frac{1}{2}$

   Certain   0

   Evens   1

2. Write down the probability of:
   a) throwing a head on a fair coin
   b) rolling a 6 on a fair ordinary dice
   c) rolling a 7 on a fair ordinary dice.

3. The table shows the probabilities for a biased spinner. Calculate the probability that the spinner lands on blue.

Red	0.42
Blue	
Yellow	0.14
Green	0.37

Further Probability

Combined Events

A **sample space diagram** can be used to show the possible outcomes from two events, e.g. tossing a coin and throwing a dice.

		Dice					
		1	2	3	4	5	6
Coin	Head	Head, 1	Head, 2	Head, 3	Head, 4	Head, 5	Head, 6
	Tail	Tail, 1	Tail, 2	Tail, 3	Tail, 4	Tail, 5	Tail, 6

P(head and 3) = $\frac{1}{12}$

P(tail and odd) is $\frac{3}{12} = \frac{1}{4}$

Example 1

A coin is tossed twice. Work out the probability of getting two heads.

Solution

> **Problem Solving**
> Tossing a coin twice is two events, so list all the possible outcomes. Alternatively you could use a sample space diagram.

Listing the possible outcomes:

Head and head   ← One of four possible outcomes

Head and tail

Tail and head

Tail and tail

So P(two heads) = $\frac{1}{4}$

Example 2

A fair coin is tossed and a fair dice is thrown. Work out the probability of getting a tail and a 3.

Solution

Listing the possible outcomes:

H1, H2, H3, H4, H5, H6

T1, T2, T3, T4, T5, T6

Tail and 3 is one of 12 possible outcomes.

So P(tail and 3) = $\frac{1}{12}$

Key Words   Sample space diagram

Theoretical Probability and Relative Frequency

Probability based on:
- equally likely outcomes is called **theoretical probability**, e.g. P(head on a fair coin) = $\frac{1}{2}$, as it's assumed that there are two equally likely outcomes (heads and tails)

- the results of an experiment is called **experimental probability** or **relative frequency**:

Relative frequency	$=$	frequency of a particular outcome / total number of trials

$$\text{Relative frequency} = \frac{\text{frequency of a particular outcome}}{\text{total number of trials}}$$

A larger number of trials should give a more reliable result.

Expectation

Expectation is the number of times you would expect an event to happen based on the relative frequency or theoretical probability.

Example 1

A fair dice is rolled 180 times.

How many times would you expect to roll a 6?

Solution

$P(6) = \frac{1}{6}$

So the expected number of sixes is $\frac{1}{6} \times 180$
= 30 times

Example 2

A five-sided spinner is spun 100 times. Here are the results:

1	2	3	4	5
16	23	32	12	17

a) Write down the relative frequency of landing on the number 4.

Solution
The spinner lands on the number 4 twelve times out of 100, so the relative frequency is $\frac{12}{100}$

b) Do you think the spinner is biased? Give a reason for your answer.

Problem Solving

Compare the relative frequency with the theoretical probability or look at the expectation for the outcomes based on theoretical probability.

Solution
If the spinner is fair, you would expect it to land on each number 20 times (out of 100) but here it lands on 3 thirty-two times. So it appears the spinner is biased because it's more likely to land on 3 than on the other numbers.

Quick Test

1. Two fair dice are rolled. Work out the probability of a total score of 7.
2. 50 drawing pins are dropped on the floor. 18 land with the point up.
   a) Write down the relative frequency of the pins landing point up.
   b) How many would you expect to land point up if 200 drawing pins are dropped?

Exam Practice Questions

You may wish to answer these questions on a separate piece of paper so that you can show full working out, which you will be expected to do in the exam.

 1. Put the probability words in order starting with the least likely. **(1)**

Even chance   Certain   Impossible   Unlikely   Likely

2. 20 boys were asked to name their favourite sport. Here are the results:

Football	Cricket	Rugby	Swimming	Football
Football	Cricket	Rugby	Football	Cricket
Rugby	Rugby	Swimming	Football	Rugby
Football	Football	Cricket	Rugby	Cricket

a) Complete the table for these results. **(2)**

Favourite Sport	Tally	Frequency
Football		
Cricket		
Rugby		
Swimming		

b) Which sport was chosen by most boys? **(1)**

c) Show the results on a bar chart. **(3)**

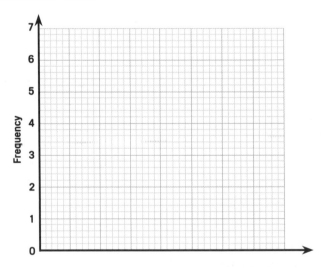

3. The mode of four numbers is 8. The median is 9. The mean is 10.

Work out the four numbers. **(3)**

4. The test scores of 15 people are shown.

17   12   25   28   16   37   11   29   34   17   22   25   12   20   19

a) On a separate piece of paper, put the results into an ordered stem and leaf diagram. Remember to complete a key. **(3)**

b) Work out the median score. **(1)**

c) Work out the range of the scores. **(1)**

5. A bag contains white, blue and red counters. A counter is chosen at random from the bag.

The probability of choosing white is double the probability of choosing red.

The probability of choosing blue is three times the probability of choosing red.

a) Work out the probability that a red counter is chosen. **(3)**

b) Jon says that there are exactly 10 counters in the bag. Explain why he must be wrong. **(1)**

6. The scatter graph shows the number of driving tests taken to pass and the number of hours of lessons for 13 students.

Copy the graph.

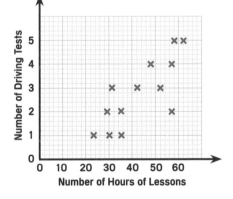

a) One of the students had more hours than normal for the number of tests taken. Circle this point on the graph and give a reason why it should be ignored. **(2)**

b) Draw a line of best fit on your graph. **(1)**

c) Describe the relationship between the number of tests taken to pass and the number of hours of lessons. **(1)**

Answers

Quick Tests

Basic Number Work (pages 4–5)

1. 1280
2. 500
3. **a)** 1253 **b)** 134 **c)** 1170 **d)** 153

Positive and Negative Numbers (pages 6–7)

1. **a)** –7 **b)** 9 **c)** –2 **d)** –2 **e)** 12 **f)** –18 **g)** –6 **h)** 3

Rounding (pages 8–9)

1. **a)** **i)** 18.7 **ii)** 18.73 **iii)** 20 **iv)** 19
   b) **i)** 0.1 **ii)** 0.07 **iii)** 0.07 **iv)** 0.073
   c) **i)** 2436.5 **ii)** 2436.52 **iii)** 2000 **iv)** 2400
2. **a)** 10 **b)** 20 **c)** 2000

Multiples and Factors (pages 10–11)

1. **a)** 14 **b)** 130 **c)** 75
2. $60 = 2 \times 2 \times 3 \times 5 = 2^2 \times 3 \times 5$
3. **a)** 40 **b)** 28 **c)** 18
4. **a)** 4 **b)** 5 **c)** 6

Fractions (pages 12–13)

1. **a)** $4\frac{7}{12}$ **b)** $1\frac{7}{20}$ **c)** 2 **d)** $1\frac{49}{65}$
2. £40
3. $\frac{1}{20}$

Decimals (pages 14–15)

1. **a)** 0.4 **b)** $0.\dot{4}$ **c)** $0.\dot{2}3076\dot{9}$
2. 9.78   9.87   10.02   10.3   10.39   10.9
3. **a)** 54.6 **b)** 0.81 **c)** 85.5 **d)** 6.1

Percentages (pages 16–17)

1. **a)** 0.4
   b) 90%
   c) $\frac{7}{20}$
2. **a)** 180 grams
   b) £16.80
3. 5%

Powers and Roots (pages 18–19)

1. **a)** 144 **b)** 27 **c)** 13 **d)** 10
2. **a)** 3^8 **b)** 8^3 **c)** 5^6

Ratio (pages 20–21)

1. **a)** 1 : 7 **b)** 3 : 2 **c)** 1 : 20 **d)** 5 : 1
2. **a)** 1 : 2 **b)** 9
3. £16 and £20
4. 90 kg

Proportion (pages 22–23)

1. 60 mph
2. **a)** $480 **b)** £312.50
3. **a)** €960 **b)** £666.66 or £666.67

Basic Algebra (pages 24–25)

1. 50°F
2. **a)** $5x$ **b)** $-4x + 7y$ **c)** $-2x^2 + 9xy$ **d)** $7x - z$
3. **a)** 5 **b)** $15\frac{1}{2}$ **c)** $-2\frac{1}{2}$
4. **a)** $x = \frac{y + 4}{5}$ **b)** $x = \frac{y}{3} - 2$ or $x = \frac{y - 6}{3}$

Working with Brackets & Trial and Improvement (pages 26–27)

1. **a)** $10x + 15$ **b)** $12x - 6y$ **c)** $x^2 - 7x$ **d)** $2x^2 + 4xy - 6xz$
2. **a)** $3(x + 2)$ **b)** $2(2x + 5y)$
   c) $4x(2x - 3)$ **d)** $5x(3y - 2x)$
3. **a)** 2.7 **b)** 2.8 or 0.6 or –3.4 **c)** 2.8 or 0.1 or –2.9

Linear Equations (pages 28–29)

1. **a)** $x = 4$ **b)** $x = 3$ **c)** $x = 10$ **d)** $x = 15$
2. **a)** $x = 3$ **b)** $x = 2$ **c)** $x = -1.25$ **d)** $x = -3$
3. **a)** $x = -7$ **b)** $x = 2$ **c)** $x = 3$ **d)** $x = 6$
4. **a)** $x = 2$ **b)** $x = 4$ **c)** $x = 7$ **d)** $x = \frac{1}{2}$

Patterns and Sequences (pages 30–31)

1. **a)**
   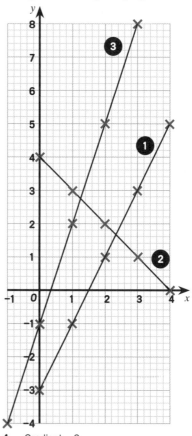
   b) 21
   c) Pattern 24
2. **a)** **i)** 20, 23 **ii)** $3n + 2$ **iii)** 62
   b) **i)** 30, 34 **ii)** $4n + 6$ **iii)** 86

Straight Line Graphs (pages 32–33)

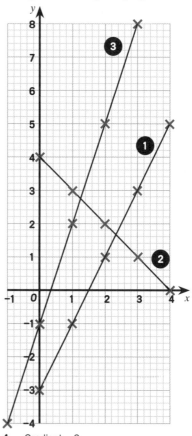

4. Gradient = 3

Linear Inequalities and Quadratic Graphs (pages 34–35)

1. **a)**
   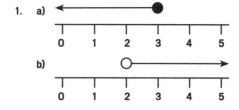
   b)

c)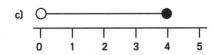

2. **a)** $x > 4$ **b)** $x \leqslant 3$ **c)** $x \geqslant 1.5$

3.

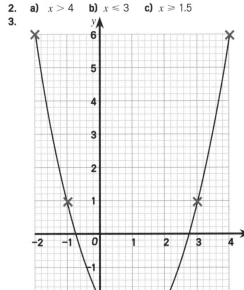

Real-life Graphs (pages 36–37)

1. **a)**

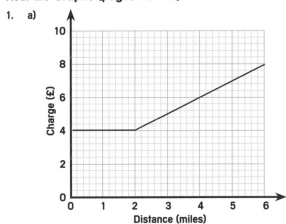

b) £7

2. **a)** $240 – $250 **b)** £240 – £260

3. **a)** B to C as it is the steepest line
b) 40 miles
c) Stopped (horizontal line)
d) 5 mph

Symmetry and Shapes (pages 42–43)

1.
E	**a)** 1	**b)** 1
I	**a)** 2	**b)** 2
Z	**a)** 0	**b)** 2
B	**a)** 1	**b)** 1
S	**a)** 0	**b)** 2
T	**a)** 1	**b)** 1
V	**a)** 1	**b)** 1
W	**a)** 1	**b)** 1

Congruency, Similarity and 3-D Shapes (pages 44–45)

1. **a)** E; J **b)** H **c)** G **d)** F
2. 5 faces, 8 edges and 5 vertices

Angles and Parallel Lines (pages 46–47)

1. **a)** 126°; allied angles
b) 47°; angles on a straight line and alternate (or corresponding) angles
c) 21°; angles on a straight line and alternate (or corresponding) angles

Angles of Polygons (pages 48–49)

1. **a)** Exterior 45°, interior 135°
b) Exterior 36°, interior 144°

Perimeter and Area (pages 50–51)

1. **a)** **i)** 12 cm **ii)** 7 cm²
b) **i)** 12 cm **ii)** 5 cm²
2. 24 cm² – 25 cm²
3. **a)** Any suitable answer, e.g.

b) Any suitable answer, e.g.

c) Any suitable answer, e.g.

4. **a)** 54 cm² **b)** 62 cm² **c)** 132 cm²

Areas of Triangles and Quadrilaterals (pages 52–53)

1. **a)** 8.05 cm² **b)** 12.65 cm² **c)** 10.08 cm²

Circumference and Area of Circles (pages 54–55)

1. **a)** **i)** 29.5 cm **ii)** 69.4 cm²
b) **i)** 19.2 cm **ii)** 29.2 cm²
c) **i)** 15.1 cm **ii)** 18.1 cm²
2. **a)** **i)** 10π cm **ii)** 25π cm²
b) **i)** 12π cm **ii)** 36π cm²

Plan and Elevation (pages 56–57)

1. **a)** **i)** **ii)** **iii)**
b) **i)** **ii)** **iii)**
c) **i)** **ii)** **iii)**

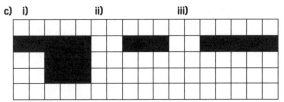

(Accept elevations in either order)

Answers

Volumes of Prisms (pages 58–59)

1. **a)** 60 cm³   **b)** 491 cm³   **c)** 42 cm³

Pythagoras' Theorem (pages 60–61)

1. **a)** 17 cm   **b)** 8.06 cm   **c)** 6.24 cm

Transformations (pages 62–63)

1. **a) and b)**

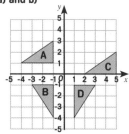

    c) Rotation 90° anticlockwise about O
    d) Reflection in the y-axis (or $x = 0$)

Basic Measures (pages 64–65)

1. 75 grams
2. **a)** 3.4 cm   **b)** 1.7 cm
3. **a)** 37°   **b)** 208°
4. **a)** 13.53   **b)** 51 minutes   **c)** 13.16 and 13.53   **d)** 15.28

Conversion and Estimation (pages 66–67)

1. **a)** 11 pounds   **b)** 24 km   **c)** 18 litres
2. **a)** Kilometres   **b)** Litres   **c)** Grams

Constructions (pages 68–69)

1. Triangle drawn to scale with lengths accurate to ±1 mm

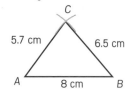

2.

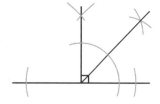

Bearings and Loci (pages 70–71)

1. **a)**    **b)** 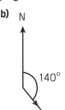   **c)**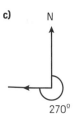

2. **a)**

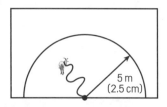

    b)

Handling Data Cycle and Questionnaires (pages 76–77)

1. **Any suitable answer, e.g.** Give each person 10 spellings; record the results; work out the mean number correct for boys and girls separately; compare the means and decide if there is any significant difference in the results.
2. It's a leading question as "Do you agree" is showing bias. It's not possible to say "Don't know".

Averages and Range (pages 78–79)

1. Mode = 9; Median = 4; Mean = 5; Range = 8
2. Modal class is $2 < x \leqslant 4$; class containing median is $2 < x \leqslant 4$; estimate of mean is 3.67

Collecting and Sorting Data (pages 80–81)

1. **a)**

    1 | 1 2 2 2 4 5 8
    2 | 2 5 5 8

    Key: 1|1   represents 11 cm

    b) Mode = 12 cm; Median = 15 cm; Range = 17 cm

2. **a)** 13   **b)** $\frac{6}{29}$

Representing Data (pages 82–83)

1. **a)** 10 boys   **b)** 5 boys

Probability (pages 84–85)

1.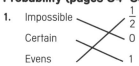

2. **a)** $\frac{1}{2}$ or 0.5   **b)** $\frac{1}{6}$ **c)** 0
3. 0.07

Further Probability (pages 86–87)

1. $\frac{1}{6}$
2. **a)** $\frac{18}{50}$ or $\frac{9}{25}$ or 0.36   **b)** 72

Answers

Exam Practice Questions

*Key: M are marks for method (e.g. **M1** means 1 mark for method); A are accuracy marks (e.g. **A1** means 1 mark for accuracy); B are independent marks that don't require method to be shown (e.g. **B2** means 2 independent marks); C are marks for quality of written communication (e.g. **C1** means 1 QWC mark).*

You're encouraged to show your working out, as you may be awarded marks for method even if your final answer is wrong. Full marks can be awarded where a correct answer is given without working being shown but if a question asks for working out, you must show it to gain full marks. If you use a correct method that isn't shown in the mark scheme below, you would still gain full credit for it.

Number and Algebra (pages 38–41)

1. **B1 a)** 2018
   B1 b) One thousand and seventy
   B1 c) 390
2. **M1** 58 − 14 + 27
   A1 71
   A1 9
3. **B1 a)** 9
   B1 b) 13
   B1 c) 27
4. **B1 a)**

   M1 b) 2 × 10 + 3 or 5, 7, 9, 11, 13 …
   A1 23
   B1 c) **Any valid reason, e.g.** all answers are odd, 84 is even
5. **B1 a)** $7x$
   M1 b) 3 × 8 + 5 × −4 or 24 − 20
   A1 4
6. **B1 a)** $x = 50$
   M1 b) $3x = 16 + 2$ or $3x = 18$
   A1 $x = 6$
   M1 c) $8x + 20 = −28$ or $2x + 5 = −7$
   M1 $8x = −28 − 20$ or $8x = −48$
   or $2x = −7 − 5$ or $2x = −12$
   A1 $x = −6$
7. **B1 a)** (3, 4)
   b)

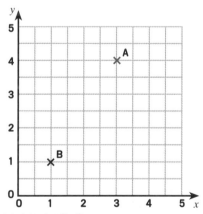

   B1 Point plotted at (1, 1)
   B2 c) (2, 2.5) **(B1 for each coordinate)**

8. **B2 a)** −4 and 2 **(B1 for each value)**
   b)

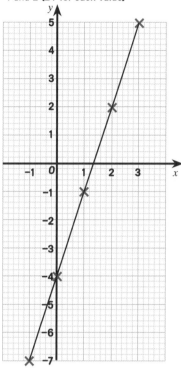

   B2 Fully correct graph **(B1 for at least three points plotted correctly)**
9. **M1** Fridge World:
   480 ÷ 3 or £160 or 480 − 160
   M1 Fridge Bargains:
   12 × 25 or £300
   M1 The Electric Store:
   $\frac{20}{100}$ × 300 or 0.2 × 300 or £60
   A2 £320, £340, £360 **(A1 for any two correct prices)**
   C1 Fridge World (is the cheapest)

   To score the quality of written communication mark you must have shown the method for each calculation.

10. **M1 a)** 5 × 6 + 3 or 30 + 3
    A1 33
    M1 b) 5 × 7 + 3 = 38 or 5 × 8 + 3 = 43 or 5 × 9 + 3 = 48
    A1 No, with working shown or reason given, e.g. $5n = 44$ doesn't give a whole number answer.

    There are lots of valid reasons for answering this part, e.g. 8th term = 43, 9th term = 48 or 47 is not 3 more than a multiple of 5, as it's 2 more than a multiple of 5.

11. **M1 a)** $\frac{16\,500 − 6900}{3}$
    A1 £3200
    M1 b) 6900 − 3200
    A1 £3700
12. **M1 a)** Factors of 42 shown, e.g. 42 = 6 × 7
    or 42 = 3 × 14 or 42 = 2 × 21
    May be on a factor tree, e.g.

    A1 2 × 3 × 7
    B1 b) $2^2 × 3^2 × 7^2$

Answers

13. **M1 a)** 15 000 − 5040 or £9960
or 14 400 − 8100 or £6300

   M1 $\frac{20}{100}$ × 9960 or $\frac{20}{100}$ × 6300

   A1 £1992 and £1260

   C1 £1992 − £1260 = £732 and Harry

   Remember to answer the question by stating clearly who pays most tax.

   M1 b) 15 000 − 1992 or 14 400 − 1260

   C1 £13 008 and £13 140
   Kim takes home £132 more.

   Remember to answer the question by stating clearly who takes home most pay.

Geometry and Measures (pages 72–75)

1. **B1 a)** 4 cm²
   M1 b) Attempt to count edges, e.g. 3 + 2 + …
   A1 10 cm
2. **a)**

   B1 Fully correct

   b)

   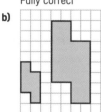

   B2 Fully correct **(B1 for at least three correct lengths)**
3. **B1** 2
4. **M1 a)** 180° − 90° − 43° or 90° − 43°
   A1 47°
   M1 b) 360° − 85° − 110° − 65° or 100°
   M1 180° − 100°
   A1 80°
5. **M1** $\frac{1}{2}$ × 6.8 × 4.2

   A1 14.28 cm²
6. **M1** $\frac{1}{2}$ (9 + 4) × 5

   A1 32.5 cm²
7. **M1 a)** $x + 34° = 47°$ or $x = 47° − 34°$
   A1 $x = 13°$
   M1 b) $y = 180° − 34°$ or $y = 133° + 13°$
   A1 $y = 146°$
8. **M1** π × 4 × 4 or π × 4²
   A1 50.26…
   B1 50.3 cm² **(Follow through any incorrect answer correctly rounded to 1 d.p. Accept 50.2cm² if π = 3.14 used.)**

   It's important that you write down your answer to more than 1 decimal place before rounding, in case you have made an error in your calculation.

9. **a)**

   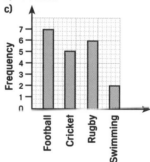

   B2 Fully correct sketch **(B1 for any correctly labelled line)**
   M1 b) $PR^2 = 20^2 + 25^2$ or $PR^2 = 400 + 625$ or $PR^2 = 1025$
   M1 $PR = \sqrt{1025}$
   A1 PR = 32 miles or PR = 32.0 miles
10. **B1** Rotation

    B1 90° clockwise or $\frac{1}{4}$ turn clockwise

    B1 About O or about (0, 0)
11. **M1** $\frac{1}{2}$ × 2 × π × 4.2 or 13.18… or 13.19…

    M1 $\frac{1}{2}$ × 2 × π × 4.2 + 4.2 + 4.2 or 21.58… or 21.59…

    A1 21.59 cm
12. **M1** Volume of cylinder = π × 12 × 12 × 30
    A1 Answer in range 13 564 to 13 574
    M1 Area of base of cuboid = 18 × 16 or 288
    M1 π × 12 × 12 × 30 = 18 × 16 × height of metal

    or height of metal = $\frac{\pi × 12 × 12 × 30}{18 × 16}$

    A1 Height of metal = 47.1… cm or 47 cm

Statistics and Probability (pages 88–89)

1. **B1** Impossible, Unlikely, Even chance, Likely, Certain
2. **a)**

Favourite Sport	Tally	Frequency
Football	ℍℍ II	7
Cricket	ℍℍ	5
Rugby	ℍℍ I	6
Swimming	II	2

   B1 Correct tallies
   B1 Correct frequencies
   B1 b) Football
   c)

   ```
   7 ┤ █
   6 ┤ █      █
   5 ┤ █  █   █
   4 ┤ █  █   █
   3 ┤ █  █   █
   2 ┤ █  █   █   █
   1 ┤ █  █   █   █
   0 ┴─────────────────
       Football Cricket Rugby Swimming
   ```
   (Frequency on vertical axis)

   B1 Labels on horizontal scale
   B1 Bars at correct heights
   B1 Fully correct with equal gaps between bars
3. **B3** 8, 8, 10, 14 **(B1 for a mode of 8; B1 for a median of 9; B1 for a mean of 10)**

4. **a)**

```
1 | 1  2  2  6  7  7  9
2 | 0  2  5  5  8  9
3 | 4  7
```

Key: 1 | 1 represents a score of 11

B1   Any correct key
B1   An unordered stem and leaf or the numbers ordered
B1   Fully correct, ordered stem and leaf
B1 **b)** 20
B1 **c)** 26

5. **M1** **a)** White : Blue : Red = 2 : 3 : 1
M1   Denominator of 6 used

A1 $\dfrac{1}{6}$

B1 **b)** **Any valid reason, e.g.** $\dfrac{1}{6}$ of 10 isn't a whole number or must be a multiple of 6 counters in the bag

6. **B1** **a)** Circle around student at (57, 2)
B1   Doesn't follow the trend of the rest of the points
B1 **b)** Line of best fit drawn starting at or before (23, 1) to (35, 1) and ending at or after (58, 5) to (62, 5)
B1 **c)** The more tests taken, the more hours of lessons (positive correlation)

Maths Dictionary

G 12-hour clock – a way of measuring or writing time using am or pm.

G 24-hour clock – a way of measuring or writing time without using am or pm. The time is written as four figures, e.g. 0340 is the same as 3.40am and 1540 is the same as 3.40pm.

G Acceleration – increase in speed or velocity.

G Acute angle – an angle that lies between 0° and 90°.

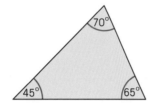

G Adjacent side – the side next to the angle or side being considered.

N Algebra – the part of mathematics which uses letters or symbols to stand for numbers.

N Algebraic expression – a statement that uses letters as well as numbers.

G Allied angles – angles that add up to 180°.

G Alternate angles – angles formed when two or more lines are cut by a transversal. If the lines are parallel then alternate angles are equal.

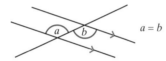

$$a = b$$

G Angles at a point – angles that meet at the same point and add up to 360°.

G Angles on a straight line – two or more angles, at the same point on a straight line, that add up to 180°.

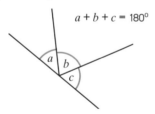

$$a + b + c = 180°$$

N Approximation – an answer that is nearly correct but not exact.

G Arc – a curve forming part of the circumference of a circle.

G Area – the surface of a shape or object is called its area.

N S Ascending – going up in order from smallest to largest.

S Average – a single number that represents or typifies a collection of values.

G Average speed – the total distance travelled divided by the total time.

$$\text{Average speed} = \frac{\text{total distance travelled}}{\text{total journey time}}$$

N Balance – keeping one side of an equation the same as the other side.

S Bar chart – a chart that uses bars of equal width to represent discrete data.

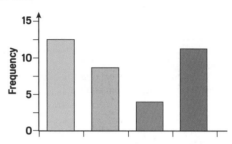

G Bearing – the direction measured clockwise from a North line at a fixed point. A bearing has three digits (for angles less than 100°, a zero, or zeros, is placed in front, e.g. 025°).

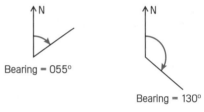

Bearing = 055°

Bearing = 130°

S Bias – a tendency either towards or away from some value; a question that invites a particular response, e.g. Do you agree that smoking is bad for you?

N BIDMAS – an acronym that helps you remember the order of operations: Brackets, Indices and roots, Division and Multiplication, Addition and Subtraction.

G Bisector – a line that divides a line, angle or area exactly in half.

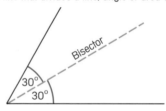

N Cancel – simplifying a fraction by dividing the numerator and denominator by a common factor.

G Capacity – the amount of space in a container or the amount of liquid it will hold.

G Centre – the middle point of something, e.g. the fixed point at the middle of a circle or a sphere.

G Centre of enlargement – the point from which the enlargement happens.

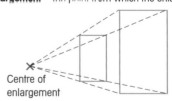

Centre of enlargement

G Centre of rotation – the point around which a shape can rotate.

S Certain – to be certain about something is to be absolutely sure that it will happen, e.g. if an event is certain, its probability equals 1.

N Change the subject – rearranging a formula to leave one variable on its own.

G Chord – a line joining two points on the circumference of a circle.

Ⓖ Circle – a shape with every point on its edge at a fixed distance from the centre.

Ⓖ Circumference – the distance all the way round the outline of a circle.

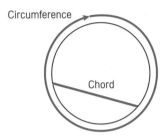

Circumference / Chord

Ⓢ Class – the grouping of large amounts of data into different classes.

Ⓢ Class interval – the width of a class or group, e.g. 0 g < mass of spider ⩽ 10 g.

Ⓝ Coefficient – a number or letter multiplying an algebraic term.

Ⓝ Common factor – a factor that is shared by two or more numbers.

Ⓝ Common multiple – a multiple that is shared by two or more numbers.

Ⓢ Composite bar chart – a bar chart that combines two or more groups of data into a single bar.

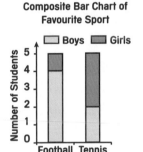

Composite Bar Chart of Favourite Sport

Ⓖ Cone – a shape with a plane circular face, a curved surface and one vertex.

Ⓖ Congruent – exactly alike in shape and size.

Ⓝ Consecutive – continuous or following in order, e.g. the numbers 1, 2, 3… are consecutive.

Ⓖ Construction – an accurate drawing of a shape using a combination of ruler, protractor and a pair of compasses.

Ⓝⓢ Continuous data – data that can take any value within a given range, e.g. length and time.

Ⓖ Conversion – changing from one measure to another, e.g. metric to imperial.

Ⓝⓖ Conversion graph – a graph used to convert from one unit to another and back again.

Ⓝⓖ Coordinate – a set of two numbers used to determine the position of a point on a graph, e.g. (3, 4).

Ⓢ Correlation – the relationship between the numerical values of two variables, e.g. there is a positive correlation between the numbers of shorts sold as temperature increases; there is a negative correlation between the age and the value of cars.

Ⓖ Corresponding angles – angles formed when a transversal cuts across two or more lines. When the lines are parallel corresponding angles are equal.

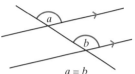

$a = b$

Ⓖ Cross-section – the shape of a slice through a solid.

Ⓖ Cube – a solid figure with six square faces.

Ⓝ Cube number – a number that is the product of three equal numbers, e.g. $4^3 = 64$

Ⓝ Cube root – the cube root of a number is a number which, when cubed, gives the original number, e.g. $\sqrt[3]{64} = 4$

Ⓖ Cuboid – a 3-D shape with six rectangular faces.

Ⓖ Cylinder – a prism with a circular cross-section.

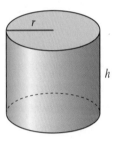

Ⓢ Data – a collection of numbers or information.

Ⓢ Data collection sheet – a sheet or log that is used to collect data.

Ⓖ Decagon – a 10-sided polygon.

Ⓝⓖ Decimal place – the position of a digit after the decimal point.

Ⓖ Degree – a unit of measurement of temperature; a degree is also a unit of measurement of angles, e.g. a complete revolution is 360 degrees.

Ⓝ Denominator – the bottom number of a fraction.

Ⓝⓢ Descending – going down in order from largest to smallest.

Ⓖ Diameter – a straight line across a circle, from circumference to circumference and passing through the centre.

Ⓝ Digit – any of the 10 numerals from 0 to 9.

Ⓝ Direct proportion – two values or measurements may vary in direct proportion, i.e. if one increases, then so does the other.

Ⓝ Directed number – a number that is given a '+' or '−' sign.

Ⓝⓖ Direction – the line along which anything lies, faces or moves.

Ⓝⓢ Discrete data – data that can only have certain values in a given range, e.g. number of goals scored, shoe sizes.

Ⓖ Distance – the length of the path between two points.

Maths Dictionary

N G Distance-time graph – a graph that shows how distance varies with time.

G Edge – where two or more faces meet on an object.

G Enlargement – a transformation of a plane figure or solid object that increases the size of the figure or object by a scale factor but leaves it the same shape.

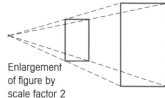

Enlargement of figure by scale factor 2

S Equally likely – the same chance (probability) of two events occurring.

N Equation – a number sentence where one side is equal to the other.

G Equidistant – a point the same distance from two or more other points.

G Equilateral – a 2-D or 3-D shape with all sides of equal length.

N Equivalent fraction – one fraction that has the same value as another fraction, e.g. $\frac{1}{2}$ and $\frac{2}{4}$ are equivalent fractions.

N G Estimate – an approximation of an actual value.

S Even chance – a probability of 0.5

N Even number – a number that when divided by 2 gives no remainder, e.g. 2, 10, 54.

S Event – something that happens, e.g. tossing a coin.

N G Exchange rate – the rate at which the currency of one country is exchanged for that of another.

N Expand (brackets) – to expand brackets means to multiply them out to get an expression without brackets.

S Expectation – the number of times you would expect an event to happen based on relative frequency (experimental probability) or theoretical probability.

S Experiment – a test or a trial.

N Expression – see **Algebraic expression**.

G Exterior angle – an angle outside a polygon, formed when a side is extended.

Exterior angle

G Face – the flat surface or side of a solid shape.

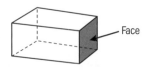

Face

N Factor – a whole number that divides exactly into a given number.

N Factorisation – finding one or more factors of a given number or algebraic expression.

S Fair – an item or event that isn't biased.

N Formula – an equation that enables you to convert or find a value using other known values, e.g. area = length × width.

N Fraction – part of a whole. Fractions can be proper, improper or mixed.

S Frequency – the number of times that something happens.

S Frequency polygon – joins the midpoints of data groups or classes in a continuous distribution.

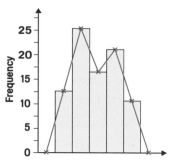

S Frequency table – an arrangement of data in a table.

G Front elevation – the 2-D view of a 3-D shape or object as seen from the front.

G Geometry – the study of angles, triangles, circles and polygons.

N G Gradient – the measure of the steepness of a slope: $\frac{\text{vertical distance}}{\text{horizontal distance}}$

S Grouped data – data that is organised into groups.

G Hemisphere – half of a sphere.

G Hexagon – a six-sided polygon.

N Highest common factor (HCF) – the highest factor shared by two or more numbers.

S Histogram – a chart that is used to show continuous data.

G Horizontal – a straight level line perpendicular to the vertical.

G Hypotenuse – the longest side of a right-angled triangle (always opposite the right angle).

S Hypothesis – a theory that is tested, by investigation, to see if it's true.

G Image – an object is transformed to give an image, e.g. after a reflection:

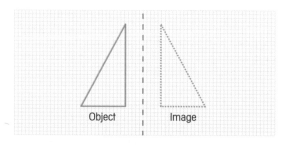

Object   Image

Ⓖ Imperial (units) – units of weight and measurement, which have generally been replaced with metric units.

Ⓢ Impossible – if an event is impossible, it can't happen, e.g. the probability of an impossible event = 0.

Ⓝ Improper fraction – a fraction in which the numerator is greater than the denominator, e.g. $\frac{9}{4}$

ⓖⓢ Increase – an enlargement or addition.

Ⓝ Index (also known as **power**) – the small digit to the top right of a number that tells us the number of times a number is multiplied by itself, e.g. 5^4 is 5 × 5 × 5 × 5; the index is 4.

Ⓝ Inequality – a statement showing two quantities that aren't equal.

Ⓝ Input – the value put into a function.

Ⓝ Integer – any whole number, positive or negative, including zero.

Ⓝ Intercept – the point where a line or graph crosses an axis.

Ⓖ Interior angle – an angle inside a polygon between two adjacent sides.

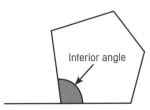

Interior angle

Ⓝ Intersection – the point at which two or more lines cross.

Ⓖ Irregular – shapes that aren't regular; sides and angles not equal.

Ⓖ Isometric drawing – a 3-D representation of an object in which the three axes are equally inclined and all lines are drawn to a given scale.

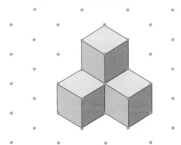

Ⓖ Isosceles – a triangle with two sides of equal length and two equal angles.

ⓖⓢ Key – a guide on a statistical chart that tells you what each symbol means.

Ⓖ Kite – a quadrilateral with two pairs of equal adjacent sides, one pair of equal opposite angles and diagonals intersecting at right angles.

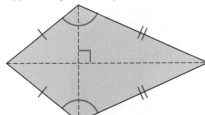

Ⓝ Least (lowest) common multiple (LCM) – the lowest number that is a multiple of two or more numbers.

Ⓢ Likely – if an event is likely it is probable, e.g. a likely event will have a probability between 0.5 and 1.

Ⓝ Like terms – terms in algebra that are the same, apart from their numerical coefficients, e.g. $2d$ and $8d$.

ⓝⓢ Limit – a boundary, or the ultimate quantity or extent of something.

Ⓢ Line graph – a graph where all the plotted points are joined by straight lines, e.g. a graph showing a hospital patient's temperature.

Ⓢ Line of best fit – a line (usually straight) drawn through the points of a scatter diagram, showing the trend and enabling you to estimate new values using original information.

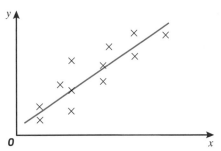

Ⓖ Line of symmetry – a line about which a shape or pattern has reflection symmetry; the two halves are mirror images of each other.

Ⓖ Line symmetry – the symmetry of a 2-D shape, giving two equal halves.

Ⓝ Linear equation – an equation that has no variable above the power 1, e.g. $y = 5x + 2$ is a linear equation.

Ⓝ Linear graph – a graph of a linear function, where all plotted points lie on a straight line.

Ⓝ Linear inequality – involves a linear expression in two variables by using any of the relational symbols such as $<$, $>$, $\leq$ or $\geq$.

Ⓖ Locus (plural: loci) – the locus of a point is the path taken by the point following a rule or rules.

ⓝⓖ Magnitude – the size of something.

Ⓖ Major sector – the larger section of the circle between two radii and an arc.

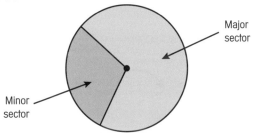

Ⓖ Major segment – the larger section of the circle between a chord and an arc.

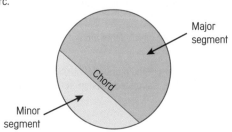

Ⓢ Mean – an average value found by dividing the sum of a set of values by the number of values.

Ⓖ Measure – to find the size, quantity or degree of something.

Maths Dictionary

Ⓢ Median – the middle item in an ordered sequence of items.

Ⓖ Metric (units) – units of weight and measure based on a number system in multiples of 10.

Ⓖ Midpoint – the point that divides a line into two equal parts.

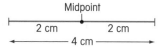

Ⓖ Minor sector – the smaller section of the circle between two radii and an arc (see **Major sector**).

Ⓖ Minor segment – the smaller section of the circle between a chord and an arc (see **Major segment**).

Ⓖ Mirror line – see **Line of symmetry**.

Ⓝ Mixed number – a whole number together with a proper fraction.

Ⓢ Modal class – the largest class in a grouped frequency table.

Ⓢ Mode – the most frequently occurring value in a data set.

Ⓝ Multiple – if one number divides exactly into another number, the second is a multiple of the first.

Ⓢ Multiple bar chart – a bar chart that shows two or more groups of data side by side.

ⓃⒼ Multiplier – the number by which another number is multiplied.

Ⓝ Multiply out – see **Expand**.

Ⓢ Mutually exclusive events – two or more events that can't happen at the same time, e.g. throwing a head and throwing a tail with the same toss of a coin are mutually exclusive events.

ⓃⒼⓈ Negative number – a number less than zero.

Ⓖ Net – a surface that can be folded into a solid.

Ⓝ nth term – the general term of a number sequence.

Ⓝ Number line – a line with a scale, showing numbers in order.

Ⓝ Numerator – the number above the line in a fraction.

Ⓖ Object – a shape.

Ⓖ Obtuse angle – an angle that lies between 90° and 180°.

Ⓖ Octagon – an eight-sided polygon.

Ⓝ Odd number – a number that when divided by 2 gives a remainder of 1, e.g. 1, 17, 83.

Ⓖ Opposite side – the side opposite the angle being worked on in a triangle.

ⓃⓈ Order – the arrangement into which items are put in ascending or descending sequence.

Ⓖ Order of rotational symmetry – the number of positions where a shape looks the same when it's rotated through 360°.

ⓃⒼ Origin – the point, with coordinates (0, 0), where the x-axis and y-axis cross.

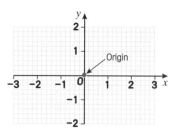

Ⓢ Outcome – the result of an event.

ⓃⒼ Parallel – lines that stay the same distance apart and never meet.

Ⓖ Parallelogram – a quadrilateral with two pairs of equal sides. Opposite sides are parallel and equal in length and the diagonals bisect each other.

Ⓖ Pentagon – a five-sided polygon.

Ⓝ Percentage – the proportion or rate per 100 parts.

Ⓝ Percentage change – the change in the proportion or rate per 100 parts.

Ⓖ Perimeter – the perimeter of an enclosed area is the boundary or edge of that area; also the length of that boundary.

ⓃⒼ Perpendicular – a line or plane that is at right angles to another line or plane.

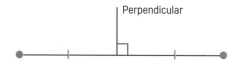

Ⓖ Perpendicular bisector – a line that is drawn at right angles to the midpoint of a line.

Ⓢ Pictogram – a chart using pictures to represent numbers of items.

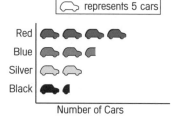

Ⓢ Pie chart – a circular chart that can be used to illustrate statistical data.

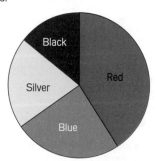

Ⓝ Place value – the place value of a digit is its value in relation to its place within the given number, e.g. in the number 167.234 the place value of 1 is 100 and the place value of 2 is $\frac{2}{10}$.

Ⓖ**Plan view** – the 2-D view of a 3-D shape or object when looking down onto it.

Ground floor of a house

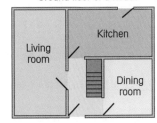

Ⓖ**Polygon** – a plane (flat) shape with many sides.

Ⓢ**Population** – the number of people who live in a certain place; any large group of items being investigated.

Ⓝ**Position-to-term rule** – the rule that links the position of the term to the term, e.g. the position-to-term rule for odd numbers is 'double the position number and subtract 1'.

ⒼⓈ**Positive number** – a number greater than zero.

Ⓝ**Power** – see **Index**.

Ⓢ**Primary data** – data collected by you for an investigation.

Ⓝ**Prime factor** – is a factor that is also a prime number.

Ⓝ**Prime number** – has only two factors, itself and 1.

Ⓖ**Prism** – a 3-D shape that has a uniform cross-section.

Hexagonal prism

Ⓢ**Probability** – the probability of an event occurring is the chance that it may happen, which can be expressed as a fraction, decimal or percentage.

$$\text{Probability} = \frac{\text{number of successful events}}{\text{total number of possible events}}$$

Ⓝ**Product** – the result of two or more numbers being multiplied together.

ⓃⒼ**Proof** – an argument or explanation that establishes the truth of a proposition.

Ⓝ**Proportion** – the relationship between things or parts of things with respect to comparative magnitude, quantity or degree.

Ⓖ**Pyramid** – a solid shape with triangular faces meeting at a vertex.

Ⓖ**Pythagoras' theorem** – the theorem which states that the square on the hypotenuse of a right-angled triangle is equal to the sum of the squares on the other two sides.

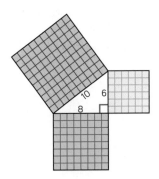

Ⓝ**Quadratic equation / expression** – an equation or expression containing unknowns with maximum power 2, e.g. $y = 2x^2 - 4x + 3$. Quadratic equations can have 0, 1 or 2 solutions.

Ⓝ**Quadratic graph** – the U-shaped graph of a quadratic equation.

Ⓖ**Quadrilateral** – a four-sided polygon.

ⓃⒼⓈ**Quantity** – an amount.

Ⓢ**Questionnaire** – a set of questions used to collect data.

Ⓖ**Radius (plural: radii)** – the distance from the centre of a circle to its circumference.

Ⓢ**Random** – something that happens by chance or without bias.

Ⓢ**Range** – the spread of data; a single value equal to the difference between the greatest and the least values.

Ⓝ**Ratio** – the ratio of A to B shows the relative amounts of two or more things and is written without units in its simplest form or in unitary form, e.g. $A:B$ is 5 : 3 or $A:B$ is 1 : 0.6

Ⓝ**Reciprocal** – the reciprocal of any number is 1 divided by the number (the effect of finding the reciprocal of a fraction is to turn it upside down, e.g. the reciprocal of $\frac{2}{3}$ is $\frac{3}{2}$).

Ⓖ**Rectangle** – a quadrilateral with two pairs of opposite, equal parallel sides and the diagonals bisecting each other; each angle is 90°.

Ⓝ**Recurring decimal** – a recurring decimal has digits that are in a repeating pattern like 0.3333 or 0.252 525.

Ⓖ**Reflection** – a transformation of a shape to give a mirror image of the original.

Ⓖ**Reflex angle** – an angle that lies between 180° and 360°.

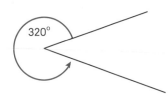

Ⓖ**Regular polygon** – a polygon that has sides of equal length and equal angles.

Ⓢ**Relative frequency** – $\dfrac{\text{frequency of a particular outcome}}{\text{total number of trials}}$

Ⓖ**Rhombus** – a quadrilateral with four equal sides but no right angles (a diamond). Opposite sides are parallel and opposite angles are equal.

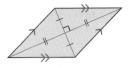

Ⓖ**Right angle** – a quarter of a revolution, or 90°.

Ⓖ**Rotation** – a geometrical transformation in which every point on a figure is turned through the same angle about a given point.

Ⓖ**Rotational symmetry** – a shape has rotational symmetry if, when rotated through 360°, there are a number of positions where the shape looks the same.

ⓃⒼ**Rounding** – replacing a number with a nearby number that is easier to work with or better reflects the precision of the data, e.g. 12 964 rounded to the nearest thousand is 13 000.

Ⓢ**Sample** – a section of a population or a group of observations.

Maths Dictionary

ⓢ Sample space diagram – a probability diagram that contains all possible outcomes of an experiment.

ⓃⒼ Scale – a marked measuring line.

Ⓖ Scale drawing – a diagram drawn to a given scale.

Ⓖ Scale factor – the ratio by which a length or other measurement is increased or decreased.

Ⓖ Scalene – a triangle that has no equal sides or angles.

ⓢ Scatter diagram – a statistical graph that compares two variables by plotting one value against the other.

ⓢ Secondary data – data used for investigation that has been collected by another person.

Ⓖ Sector – see **Major sector** and **Minor sector**.

Ⓖ Segment – see **Major segment** and **Minor segment**.

Ⓖ Semicircle – half of a circle.

Ⓝ Sequence (or **series**) – a collection of terms following a rule or pattern.

Ⓖ Side elevation – the 2-D view of a 3-D shape or object as seen from the side.

ⓃⒼ Significant figure – the number of digits in a number giving a required degree of accuracy.

Ⓖ Similar – the same shape but a different size.

Ⓝ Simplify – making something easier to understand, e.g. simplifying an algebraic expression by collecting like terms.

Ⓖ Solid – if an object has three dimensions it's known as a solid figure or solid shape, e.g. a cuboid is a solid figure.

ⓃⒼ Speed – how fast something moves.

Ⓖ Sphere – a 3-D ball shape in which all points of its surface are equidistant from its centre.

Ⓖ Square – a quadrilateral that has four equal sides and four right angles.

Ⓝ Square – to square a number is to multiply it by itself.

Ⓝ Square number – a number that is the product of two equal factors, e.g. $25 = 5^2$

Ⓝ Square root – the square root of a number is the number that, when squared, gives that number, e.g. $\sqrt{25} = 5$

ⓢ Statistics – a collection of data used for analysis.

ⓢ Stem and leaf diagram – a semi-graphical diagram used for displaying data by splitting the values.

```
1 | 0  8  9
2 | 1  2  5  5  5
3 | 0  1  2  2  4  4  7

1 | 0  represents 10 text messages
```

Ⓝ Substitution – to exchange or replace, e.g. in a formula.

Ⓖ Surface area – the area of the surface of a 3-D shape, equal to the area of the net of that shape.

ⓢ Survey – a collection of data for statistical analysis.

Ⓖ Symmetry – a 2-D figure can have rotational or line symmetry; a 3-D shape can have rotational or plane symmetry.

ⓢ Tally – to count by making marks.

Colour of Car	Tally	Frequency
Red	ЖЖ ЖЖ ǁ	12
Blue	ЖЖ ǁ	7
White	ǁǁ	3
		Total 22

Ⓖ Tangent – a straight line that touches the circumference of a circle at one point only.

Ⓝ Term – in an expression, any of the quantities connected to each other by an addition or subtraction sign.

Ⓝ Terminating decimal – a decimal fraction with a finite number of digits, e.g. 0.75

Ⓝ Term-to-term rule – a rule that links one term to the next term, e.g. the term-to-term rule for even numbers is 'add 2'.

Ⓖ Tessellation – a pattern made by fitting together plane shapes (usually regular) without gaps.

ⓢ Theoretical probability – a predicted probability; calculated using the fraction $\dfrac{\text{number of particular outcomes that can happen}}{\text{number of outcomes that are possible from the task}}$

Ⓖ Three-figure bearing – see **Bearing**.

Ⓖ Timetable – a list of the times at which certain events, such as departures and arrivals at a bus station, are expected to take place.

Ⓖ Transformation – an action such as a translation, reflection, rotation or enlargement.

Ⓖ Translation – a transformation in which all points of a plane figure are moved by the same amount and in the same direction. The movement can be described by a vector.

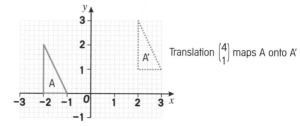

Translation $\binom{4}{1}$ maps A onto A'

Ⓖ Trapezium – a quadrilateral with just one pair of parallel sides.

ⓢ Trial – a test or an experiment.

Ⓝ Trial and improvement – a method of solving an equation by making an educated guess and then refining it step-by-step to get a more accurate answer.

Ⓖ Triangle – a three-sided polygon.

Ⓖ Triangular prism – a prism with a triangular cross-section.

ⓢ Two-way table – a data-handling table to illustrate two variables.

		Team	
	Red	Blue	Green
7	16	18	16
Year 8	15	17	16
9	15	15	15

ⓃⒼ Unit – means one, a single thing or number; the place-value position immediately to the left of the decimal point.

Ⓝ Unit fraction – a fraction with the numerator 1, e.g. $\frac{1}{3}, \frac{1}{27}$

S **Unlikely** – if the probability of an event occurring is very small, the event is unlikely to happen.

NS **Variable** – a quantity that can have many values, usually written as a letter, e.g. x, a, k.

NG **Vector** – a quantity with both magnitude and direction, e.g. velocity, force, displacement.

G **Velocity** – a more formal, and more correct, way of describing speed using both a magnitude and a direction, e.g. 30 mph towards the North.

G **Vertex** – in 2-D a point where two or more lines meet. In 3-D the corners of a shape, where the edges meet.

G **Vertical** – at right angles to the horizontal, e.g. the perpendicular bisector is vertical and at right angles to the horizontal line at its midpoint.

S **Vertical line graph** – a graph using vertical lines that can be used to represent discrete data.

G **Vertically opposite angles** – vertically opposite angles are formed when two straight lines intersect. The four angles add up to 360°.

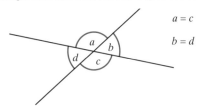

$$a = c$$
$$b = d$$

G **Volume** – the amount of space occupied by a substance or object or enclosed within a container.

N **Whole number** – an integer, or a number used for counting.

Formulae Sheet

Area of a trapezium = $\frac{1}{2}(a + b)h$

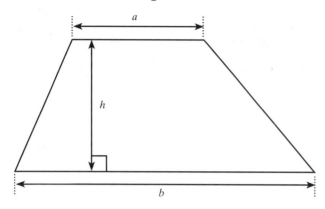

Volume of a prism = area of cross-section × length

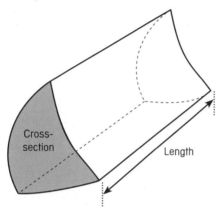